Thrivability

Breaking through to a world that works

Jean M. Russell

This book is dedicated to my children, Emory and Zoe,
for whom I imagine a thrivable world.

Published in this first edition in 2013 by:
Triarchy Press
Station Offices
Axminster
Devon. EX13 5PF
United Kingdom

+44 (0)1297 631456
info@triarchypress.net
www.triarchypress.net

A catalogue record for this book is available from the British Library.

Cover illustration and design, author photographs, and the delicious vegetation graphics at the start of each section by:
Hava Gurevich – www.hava.biz

Print ISBN: 978-1-909470-28-6

Contents

References, Notes, and Bibliography are at:
www.triarchypress.net/thrivability

Introduction

Thrivability. I first heard the word at a wiki conference in February 2007. I'd like to be able to say the effect was like lightning, but it was more like a pot slowly filling – one drop of curiosity joining another, day after day. Over time, questions began to cascade. What is this word? What does it mean? How would it be possible? Why does it feel so deeply compelling to me and others? It has taken me over like a full-blown infection of possibility. And I delight in seeing others catch the 'possibility virus' too.

Something about thriving speaks to our inner sense of harmony, abundance, greatness, generativity, aliveness, vitality, wellbeing, and right-placement. What would our lives and our society be like if we were able to say they were thriving? I want to be able to say that we are thriving. Intensely. Coming across this word was like finding the name of my homeland. The word captures all the things I want for myself, my family, my community, the organizations I work with, and the world as a whole.

People often ask me to define thrivability. Beyond defining it as 'the ability to thrive,' I struggle, as the word captures and conveys so much. Each definition seems an oversimplification. But here, in this book, I have attempted to distill the 20 years of exploration and passionate curiosity that led me first to see and then champion the idea and the reality of thrivability. Along the way, I shall describe many, major and converging shifts in many different fields – shifts that combine to make a thriving world a practical possibility. Taken together, these shifts weave a larger story of our passage from one era to another – an evolutionary phase change that we are in the midst of.

'Thrive' is rooted in the word 'thrift' but loosens it, letting go of the tightness and withholding, keeping prudence, and bursting forth with added abundance and generosity. It is that shift from the austere world of thrift to one of thriving that I am going to explore in this book.

Thrivability is not static. It is dynamic and in motion.

Thrivability is the ability for you and me to thrive, for what is around us to thrive, and for thriving to be the sum of all we do. Thrivability emerges from each of us holding the persistent intention to be generative: that is to say, to create more value than we consume. When practiced over time, this builds a world of ever-increasing possibilities.

The more I have explored, the more I believe we all want that – for ourselves and, more and more, for the world around us.

I hope you will come to see, with me, that this is neither a utopian dream nor the latest branding message from the green/sustainability movement. Instead, it is a deep call for us to shift up a level – to 'level up' – in our understanding of life in all its complexity: to be generative in a broader context than ever before.

We strive toward the greatness implicit in thriving, flourishing, plentitude.

We are in the midst of a great breakdown. In the midst of many convergent crises. And nature is always in the process of breakdown. Always in crisis.

We are also in the midst of great breakthroughs. And nature is always also in the process of breakthrough. So I see this current phase change as a great unfolding: the old order is breaking down and we are breaking through to a new order.

As part of the breakdown we are coming to recognize that the way things have been cannot continue. At the same time, 'edge-riders' are beginning to see the breakthroughs that are happening: breakthroughs to a human culture that won't just sustain life but will give rise to more abundant life – as well as recognizing those things we already do that enable more life to arise.

In these pages, I invite you to explore the concepts and breakthroughs that make it possible to realistically envision and co-create a world of wellbeing and health – a world that works better. One that works for many, many more people than the world we currently inhabit, and one that works for the ecosystems we depend on. I will also describe some of the new ways of seeing and perceiving, ways of knowing and understanding, and ways of acting and doing in the world that have transformed and inspired me while I have been exploring different emerging ideas and paradigm shifts across many disciplines. Taken together, these ways of perceiving, understanding, and doing offer us practical hope and clear paths forward.

This is not a vision of a world without death, decay, or destruction. I am not suggesting an end to suffering and loss. Loss is part of the natural cycle. And grief is a healthy response to loss. Nor am I suggesting that we can control what happens next. We can't. But we do have agency. Together, we can take actions that will make a significant difference. We don't have to stand by and passively, tragically suffer losses without purpose. Instead, let us learn to honor and grieve loss, crafting a story that honors what has been and gives courage to our next steps. This is a vision of a world where everything that decays becomes fodder for new life. Nature is our model. Life thrives. Pieces and parts may wither, be destroyed, or die, but the sum of the system can still expand. Life creates more life.

This book is about opening the space for a new story to unfold. Everyone can contribute. You already are. I invite you to rewrite the story that you tell about your own life. And from there, consider how we can together re-write a new collective story that each of us can contribute to.

~

So let me map out the book a little. After an overview of thrivability, I invite you to look first at our ways of **Perceiving** (Part I of the book). Consider how you see the world, where you're looking from and what lenses you're looking through. In Chapter 1, I explore the 'Great Unfolding' and face the gritty reality of what is. I name some of the problems and transformations we are engaging in. In Chapter 2, I look at the stories we tell about ourselves and the world we live in – and the difference those stories can make. To help make sense of the changes we are experiencing, I zoom out in Chapter 3 to look at the very big picture and to explore some ways of perceiving and changing our perspective. Chapter 4 has a brief primer on systems, where we clarify the difference between causality and correlation. Understanding this crucial distinction is the key to adjusting our course of action and expectations. It's the key to effective navigation.

In Part II, **Understanding**, I describe the tools and insights that are combining to make the possibility of thriving a more practical reality. In Chapter 5 I explore how brain science has shown us to be quite different human beings than those we thought we were and, in Chapter 6, I look at how the social revolution is shaping the emerging world today. Chapter 7 shows why information and data visualization allow us to see ourselves better – making what was once invisible now visible.

In Part III, **Doing**, I look at ways we can take action together for a more thrivable world. With Chapter 8, I explore some of the keys to creativity.

From there, Chapter 9 looks at how games can pull all of that together to enable us to collaborate and co-create our world in powerful ways. In Chapter 10 I explain the 'Action Spectrum Framework' which shows how actions that we can all take now to control, guide, and nurture have different opportunities, rewards and attribution.

The entire book is peppered with practical questions, and exercises (see the 'Try it' sections) to help bring thrivability to you, your community, your organization and our world. My goal is to help you move from insight into practice. The book is also full of references to people, other books, ideas and work that I have drawn on extensively. In place of footnotes and endnotes I have simply added everything to the resources section of the book's webpage: **triarchypress.net/thrivability**

Feel free to skip sections you feel you know already, skim to the takeaways, or play in the 'Try It' sections. Note that most of the 'Try It' questions focus on the individual – you. Transformation of organizations and systems starts with individuals who are willing to ask questions and consider things from a different point of view. I am offering questions for you that can spiral out from you to your connections, organization, and indeed to society at large.

My goal is to equip you with tools to see and act in ways that enrich your life, your community, your business, and our world.

My goal is selfish really... since I believe that enriching our world will create the world I want my children to grow up in and interact with. Maybe you want that for future generations too?

Throughout the book I will be giving attention – not to our old models of the world which are failing us now – but to the pilots and forerunners of new models that are already running and working. Old paradigms no longer make sense of everything we can perceive in the world around us. We can wring our hands with worry about that, or we can look for new models that better describe the world we find ourselves in. I invite you to look forward to the next era for humanity. Welcome to Thrivability.

Thrivability

We have been so magnificently successful at growing that it is killing us.

In *The Death of Demand*, Tom Osenton demonstrated that products, departments, organizations, and even whole sectors and industries achieve innovation saturation – their growth rates increase rapidly, hit a peak and decrease equally fast. In the process, the myth of endless economic growth collapses – shattering the dreams of infinite and perpetually growing riches. In the world of breakdown thinking, there is only collapse and the shattering of dreams. But in the world of breakthrough thinking, we can see that something better may replace the unsustainable pursuit of endless economic growth. In its place we might, for example, find ways to become sustainable consumers. We might become co-consumers or co-producers.

In the world of breakdown thinking (the pessimistic view of the world that we so often find in the media) the focus is on economic and social collapse. In breakdown thinking, the story we tell ourselves hardly encourages us to even try to play the 'game' of evolving society. In gaming terms, the challenge is too great, the individual feels too unskilled, and the rewards are too often labeled as sacrifices. I don't think we are going to get to the world we want by telling stories of scarcity, collapse and sacrifice. Of course, there have been some brilliant results driven or achieved by breakdown thinking, but that story fails to garner enthusiasm. It doesn't win over any hearts. I see so many people around me playing the game called 'stop bad things happening' – their purpose is clear and powerful and their hearts ache from the agony of being connected to so much global suffering. They are right to want to stop those things (population explosion, species extinction, climate change, environmental degradation, etc.), but I'm going to show that there is another path that will work better and achieve more.

This other path does not deny the challenges at hand or scarcity where it exists. It is more powerful because it acknowledges resources we already have, builds on successes we have already achieved, and taps into strengths we already possess. I'm going to show that there's a different game afoot. A game that invites us to 'create, share, and evolve together'; a game where we each work toward a world that works. A game that, together, we might win.

What if we play to win instead of playing not to lose?

Playing not to lose is about avoiding death and threats. It is about trying not to destroy the planet and ourselves. It is about surviving not thriving. If you are not dead, you have not lost. But what if instead we played to win? A giant epic win?

Look around at the changes that are just going to global scale now. Many of them began long ago. Some in the 1970s, 80s, and 90s. Others started a century ago or more. So we can also look around at the changes that are just beginning now and imagine how they could transform the world if they were scaled up or scaled outward. What if the small breakthroughs of today (like Walkscore) were to proliferate in the world of tomorrow?

In taking this approach I don't mean, in any way, to suggest that the tasks at hand are not monumental or that the gritty reality of today isn't riddled with potential and actual catastrophes. But I am inviting you to consider the breakthroughs just as thoroughly as the breakdowns. And once you have, I want you to decide which world you want to believe you are in. I want you to make a play for the thrivable world.

Find others who are acting as if the world is already thriving. Talk to people who tell stories about how the world is becoming ever more thrivable. Focus on creating solutions – with others. Whether they know they are part of a new era of thriving or not, there are many movements that tap into the elements of thriving discussed here.

Try it

Think of another recent breakthrough you are familiar with – or imagine one.

- ⊤ What would it take for that to be scaled up to global proportions?
- ⊤ Is it physically possible?
- ⊤ Don't worry if it is socially or financially possible, those things can be overcome with the right incentives.
- ⊤ Imagine what the world might look like in five or ten or twenty years if that breakthrough were scaled up.
- ⊤ Imagine yourself in that future. What are five things you notice about that world?

Walkscore

Take walkscore.com for example. The site/application creates a percentage rating based on how 'walkable' a location is. The score takes into account how far you have to walk to get to a restaurant, coffee shop, post office, grocery store, school, or park. It also factors in crime rates and transportation options. How does this score change the possibilities?

If I value walking over driving, the score lets me find a location to live that better fits my values. If I am considering several different locations for a business, it lets me select one where my business is most likely to thrive because it will meet the needs of the local community (for example, I can identify a neighborhood that has a low walkscore for the service I want to provide – say a grocery or a restaurant.)

If I work in local government, I might be able to tell that a neighborhood needs to cultivate particular services and offer incentives that will attract them into the area.

Walkscore makes it clear that people value being able to walk to things that serve their needs. ("Over 10 million scores viewed per day" says this is important to a lot of people.) Thus, entrepreneurs will generate businesses and officials will generate policy aligned with that value.

Walkscore makes that value measurable. Regardless of your position in relation to the walkscore (buyer, investor, official), you can track progress in the direction you want to work towards. Everyone can start playing the walkscore game. You can also build apps on the walkscore data and there are data services for further analysis.

Walkscore gamifies walkability. And when more people walk to meet their needs, we have less pollution from transportation, and people connect with others locally, weaving better local networks. Walking also encourages local discovery of stores, cultural events, and meeting places. What happens when more of the world has walkscores? How does that change decisions that businesses make about where to locate and policies that state, city, and local governments decide? Does it help people and local communities thrive? What does it make possible if taken to a global scale and if we let the game run for five years or more?

Level up!

Movements

When I started exploring the idea of thrivability, I looked around me to see where thriving might already be happening. I wondered who was working to bring about thrivability and how. If this was really a way of describing a paradigm shift, I wanted to see if there were corresponding changes to behavior in the world; if there were practices that took a radically new approach. Were there efforts out there that went beyond the sustainability story, evolving it further? Were they significant enough to take notice of? I was amazed by what I discovered. If we look at the people and groups who are pulling together, creating breakthroughs and telling new stories about how we are going to move forward, there is a broad spectrum of forward-looking pragmatic efforts in practice today:

- Focusing on solutions, we have **magazines** in the US like *Ode, Yes!* and *Good. Ode* focuses on intelligent optimists, *Good* addresses a business-driven social innovator audience, and *Yes!* presents positive action and solutions for progressive activist culture.

- The **Games for Change** movement now spreading across the world infuses change with games – that is to say playfulness and hugely motivating gamification tools – that reduce suffering and increase human aliveness and joy.

- **Transition towns** began in the UK and have spread globally. The transition town movement focuses on local decision-making and action to address carbon issues while also building community action around consensus-determined goals.

- Related, but without the organizational coherence of transition towns, the **Resilience Movement** includes a significant number of environmental and sustainability advocates who have expanded the agenda to include adaptability and agility in their survival plans and actions.

- More playfully, the do-it-yourself (DIY) and craft movement has re-awakened with *Make* magazine and the Maker Faire events which regularly see many tens of thousands of makers coming together to share both whimsical and practical DIY products and objects. Making allows for customization of the idea, production, and product. As we move from factory production to customized production in a networked environment, the **Maker Movement** forms a large, action-focused builder culture.

╤ Both the Maker Movement and the Resilience Movement offer solutions to the dilemmas wrought by our push toward globalization (which, in turn, has made us hugely dependent on goods from other countries). They include the emergence, in the last few years, of **Etsy**, which allows individual makers to sell their makings to a wide and growing audience of buyers. Making isn't just a hobby for some.

╤ Alongside the DIY movement, MIT has spawned **Fab Labs** which have spread to more than 30 countries. Here, individuals and groups can use shared tools in a collaborative environment to make things. From 3D printers to machines that make themselves, the innovations in this space are awe-inspiring, creative, and open new pathways for production, customization, and distribution.

These are all elements of a shift from factory production to network production – where there is significantly more customization. Creativity plays here.

╤ With **eBay**, **Craigslist**, and **Freecycle**, the last decade or so has seen the rise of simple ways we can both transact and share with each other, often based on tools that enable sufficient trust between strangers. The **mesh economy** or collaborative consumption movement, as it is sometimes called, focuses on sharing resources. Sharing makes better lifestyles and businesses more accessible to many. See **Shareable**, **Ouishare**, and **Peers.org** as they soar!

╤ When we combine making with sharing, we have collaborative production! Check out the **Peer to Peer Foundation, Appropedia**, or a **TechShop** near you.

╤ **Co-working environments**, like **Citizen Space** and the social entrepreneur, co-working **HUBs** across the world, enable small and emerging businesses to have affordable office space, community connection, and generative targeted learning events (brown bag lunch talks on relevant topics or day-long workshops to enable members to build their skills).

Now that more people feel comfortable selling, sharing, and buying goods directly from each other, more people have access to goods and services through sharing then ever before. (Though our standard of living has been on the decline in the United States since the 1970s, with our dollars buying less and less in the direct sale dimension of the economy, we have begun to make up that standard-of-living decline with a rise in the quality-of-life through the pre-owned or shared dimension of the economy.)

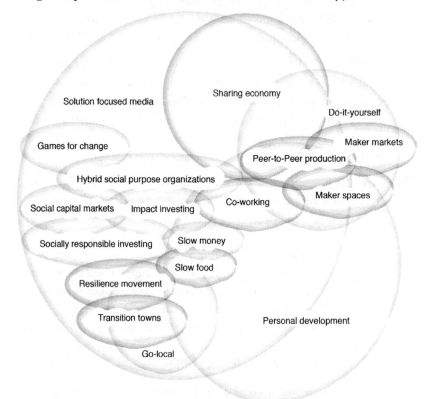

Movements

If the 1950s to 90s seemed to come with a drive for ever more speed, the **Slow Movement** wants to slow back down. Breaking away from the old 'make me as much money as possible as soon as possible' model, the Slow Money effort is putting investment capital to work on long-term projects, usually focused on local resilience. It has an older sister, the Slow Food movement.

- The Slow Movement is about going local and the '**go local**' meme also includes the burgeoning **BALLE (Business Alliance for Local Living Economies)**.

- If there ever was a radical difference between doing well and doing good, it is breaking down. And in its place, new business forms and practices are emerging where business can put purpose to work in the service of social agendas. With the expansion of **Socially Responsible Investing** and **Corporate Social Responsibility**, even businesses without an explicit social intention, driven by market demands, are shifting toward more socially beneficial practices. Sure, there is a lot of greenwashing, but that doesn't take away from the real improvements that are being achieved. Trying to spin a story that you are meeting social or environmental responsibility targets is already a step along the way to more organizations genuinely striving to achieve those targets.

- The **Social Capital Markets** space, which I have been tracking for four years now, has grown in size year after year. In parallel, each year more US states allow L3C incorporation and B corporations, organizational forms that explicitly merge purpose with profit. Even if we were to count the financial flows of all of those organizations with their legal structures designed for social good, it would be only a small portion of the larger wave of socially driven or socially compatible organizations. Many choose hybrid business forms or partner for philanthropic ends. It isn't the exception any more. Being socially and environmentally responsible and engaged is becoming the norm.

- Away from business, the field of **personal development** is also shifting us toward a more thriving world. We learn that buying stuff doesn't make us happy... and that the search for happiness leads to a search for meaning and contribution to society. It isn't just a few enlightened souls but increasingly a mass awareness amongst just about anyone in any part of American society. Hello to the world of Oprah. We know it. We might make fun of ourselves for it. Yet more people are taking action designed to move toward lives of greater meaning and purpose because of it.

Try it

T   What other movements are you aware of, or part of, that enable a thrivable world?

T   What organizations and individuals do you notice holding up a story of greater possibility?

When I look across all these movements, I am stunned by the number of people involved and the passion they have to find new ways to access resources through the sharing economy, to develop themselves through personal work, to come together to make things and work together in mutually supportive, community structures, to create and sustain better working and living environments.

All this is crucial if we are to make the hard decisions in front of us where we must often pick collective long-term benefit over short-term individual gains. While there is a thread of thrift in the sharing economy and other movements of this unfolding era, there is also a striving toward greater generativity and opening to possibility. We innovate. We expand toward thriving – not from fear or self-righteousness, but from a sense of care, connection, and the endless human drive for something greater.

Level up!

PART I: PERCEIVING

Nearly hit by a bus? Get results back from the doctor letting you know that you are in the clear – a near miss? Hear a tragic story that made you think, if not for some small decision your fate would have been the same as theirs?

When I was working with a philanthropic advisor, Drake, we talked about these moments that open people up to generous giving and purposeful living. They are powerful moments where suddenly we see the world from a different view and make massive changes to re-orient to a new true north in ourselves. Inspirational stories often have this insight moment in them. And you can't really trick people into them very easily, even though we love hearing them.

Through numerous conversations with Drake, I started to see that our way of perceiving things is like a program we are running. Disruptive events can trigger shifts in that unconscious programming. But also hearing of someone else having such a moment can be potent too. It was certainly challenging for me because I had to acknowledge with each of the stories we looked at that I wasn't aware of this programming in my life. I had to start critically examining the lenses I was viewing my own life through and I had to make adjustments. Did it really take a bus or medical tests for me to realize that I should say a heartfelt "I love you" to the people who mattered to me? Or make right my arguments quickly lest someone die, leaving that wound to haunt me?

Probably the biggest moment for me in this period changed my life dramatically. I had been struggling in my marriage. I had chosen to stay for the sake of our kids. My programming said: their happiness has to come before everything. Things shifted when I realized I needed to really live the life *I* wanted – if I was going to champion my kids to choose and live the lives *they* wanted. I needed to do it, not just tell them or read them stories about it. I couldn't ask them to live boldly if I wasn't. After that perspective shift, I radically altered my life and my parenting.

Although I was working with Drake to help more people lead purposeful lives, in the process I had to fix a lot of things in my own life. And it didn't make my life any easier for quite some time. Proceed with caution. You might end up feeling you need to change your own life, your work, and the way you engage with the world. At the same time, learning how to be in charge of your own perceptions can be really thrilling, opening up possibilities and deepening connections that matter.

Can you see the story of thriving unfolding? If you don't already see it all around you, then our first step together is to become aware of the different viewpoints from which each of us looks at the world, and the different lenses we look through – and to see how we might change them.

Are we being too myopic as a society in the view we have of the future (and the present)? In this section on perceiving, I want to equip you with doubts, so you can challenge things that you've been certain of until now. And I want to equip you with new possibilities and ways of seeing, so you can decide for yourself what story you want to tell about the world you're living in.

CHAPTER 1

The Great Unfolding: Crisis and Opportunities

A number of recent books by experts in the field confirm what many of us already suspect – that there is a financial and economic crisis at hand (although it seems to me that something remains unsaid or unnoticed about what is unfolding before us).

The Great Disruption by Paul Gilding tells of the impending and unavoidable financial and environmental crisis and offers a grand plan to change course. But the author insists that we will avoid acknowledging these problems or taking significant action until we can't ignore them any more. Only then will we act. Jared Diamond offers dire warnings in *Collapse: How Societies Choose to Fail or Succeed*, showing how the concerns that face us are similar to the concerns of other societies that have collapsed in the past. Joshua Cooper Ramo's *The Age of the Unthinkable: Why the New World Disorder Constantly Surprises Us And What We Can Do About It* acknowledges that we are participants in complex adaptive systems (more about these later) that require radically new approaches.

No matter what we call it, there is a convergence of crises at hand that involves a breakdown in the growth-focused form of capitalism.

You don't have to be a Marxist to see this; just look around and see the infectious movement of people across the political spectrum who are saying, "we've had enough." Physical infrastructure is crumbling. According to Jo Guldi of the Harvard Society of Fellows:

> "As anti-government politics choked infrastructure spending, they not only halted development but also seriously damaged the nation's skeleton. Eighty percent of the nation's dams are more than 50 years old. The American Society of Civil Engineers estimates that some 41 of these dams are at risk of causing imminent destruction of life and property. Infrastructure maintenance in the United States as a whole is behind to the degree of $1.6 trillion.

America's magnificent cage of infrastructure is like a dying coral reef, poisoned by a facile form of fiscal conservatism."

And it isn't just the tremendous infrastructure of a modernist era that has aged and crumbled. It's the systemic infrastructures our society lives upon that are disintegrating under their own weight and internal contradictions – financial, political, and social. The entire process of elections in the US became questionable in 2000 with the Bush/Kerry election. US citizens, by and large, simply don't trust the election process anymore. The education system is widely perceived to need a major overhaul. And five years of the Great Recession doesn't bode well for the current financial system, which – according to the International Monetary Fund – has seen 425 systemic financial and monetary crises around the world in the last 40 years.

As these infrastructure systems collapse, breakdown, or transform, they pull on the warp and weft of our world, opening up a new dimension that can help to extract us from the rigidity of our dualisms: capitalism/communism, dictator/democracy, left/right, male/female. I call what's happening the 'Great Unfolding' and I believe it reveals new and greater possibilities.

We have before us the perfect storm for triggering a sense of purpose: convergent catastrophes across numerous domains: economic, political, social, and environmental.

The Economic Reality

The polarizing marketplace tensions of the twentieth century – capitalism and communism; and their drivers: the political left and the political right – are coming to be recognized as useful, but only limited, improvements on what came before: feudalism. Communism may have fallen first from its inconsistencies and poorly designed incentives, but capitalism – as we have known it – teeters precariously too.

We have learned much from both approaches as we evolve through systems that better enable autonomy, mastery, and purpose – which Daniel Pink claims are the three keys to human motivation. Capitalism made more room for these three keys than communism. It enabled much more autonomy than feudalism as well as deeper specialization (which brings with it a sense of mastery). However, it is time to accommodate the human drive for a purpose that goes beyond the individual and senses something greater than ourselves.

The big idea that has been touted about capitalism, markets, and endless growth – that an abundance of things for consumers to consume leads to human progress and betterment – turns out to be a myth. The same is true of trickle-down economics – the myth that when the rich do well, they will pay for goods and services that employ the lower classes, thus cascading wealth down the financial prosperity ladder. There are numerous ways of arguing that the environment cannot continue to support economic systems based on infinite growth. These arguments use evidence based on population growth, food and water supply, money systems, health and many other issues. But I shall use one, concise, non-environmental argument to make the point. It proves the faulty logic at the heart of endless-growth capitalism. The argument is central to Tom Osenton's book *The Death of Demand*, which has solid, long-term data revealing that all companies and all products experience two growth trends during their life cycle – an uptrend and a downtrend.

When Osenton released his book in 2004, it was largely ignored. Who would want to hear the news about 'innovation saturation'? And what were investors supposed to do with this knowledge? Today, more and more people are recognizing the validity of his argument.

Osenton looks the part of a researcher focused on finding the truth rather than a troublemaker intent on proving a point or stirring anxiety. When I spoke with him in late 2009, he was all numbers, patterns, and seriousness. The first time we met, we drew furiously on the 3x5 cards I had with me that night. He would explain, then I would draw while he clarified. In 2005 his research had been validated in a study that took the revenue growth rates of the top S&P 500 corporations. He talked about having found the pattern by covering his walls with the graphs of company after company – looking not just at revenue growth, but the rate of growth. And he looked at 10-year lumps instead of quarterly fluctuations, zooming out to see a larger historic pattern. He must have seemed like a madman with his walls covered like that, but how else could he have seen in one view so much information and the pattern it contained? The scale of the project and the quiet diligence of this man impressed me.

"After experiencing a period of ever-increasing growth rates, a company hits a wall, at which time growth rates turn south at ever-decreasing rates," he says. "At this point, revenue as a profit driver loses steam and in its place cost-cutting grows in importance in order to deliver what Wall

Street demands – ever-increasing earnings. However, just as revenue as an earnings driver has its limits, so too does cost-cutting. This illusory dance can continue for many years – but make no mistake about where it's headed. And it's very important to remember that cost-cutting and job-creation are enemies that cannot possibly co-exist – especially at a maturing organization." So growth-decay companies are effectively starving themselves of resources to give the appearance of continually expanding margins. Who is in growth decay? The majority of companies listed on Wall Street.

Increasing rates of growth are a thing of the past for too much of Wall Street. The collective peak (see chart) was in the 1980s. Too many of the companies traded there have passed their growth peak – the result of innovation saturation. The Wall Street stock market was designed to generate investment in businesses that were growing, but now it contains too many companies that are no longer increasing their rates of growth. We have become so effective at growth that the time from 'start-up' to 'growth peak' is getting significantly shorter. Instead of the long slopes of growth we saw with companies like

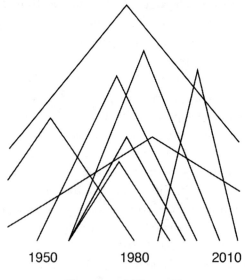

1950   1980   2010

Rates of Growth

Procter and Gamble over 100 years, we have Microsoft in 20 years, and Groupon in a couple years. The time to peak is so short in fact that even products or companies a decade old can be past their growth peak.

Another way of looking at this change is to compare the rate at which companies get bumped off the S&P 500 – the index of the 500 most valuable companies traded on the US stock market. Richard Foster has done this and, as reported in *Technology Review*:

> "What Foster found is that... Back in 1958, a company could expect to stay on the list for 61 years. These days, the average is just 18 years."

And this growth-to-decay cycle is getting faster. Infinite growth, like the 'Emperor's New Clothes,' has been shown to be an illusion. The housing crisis and the dot-com boom/bust have revealed the Wall Street Empire to be as naked as the emperor in the fairy tale. The Occupy movement has already succeeded by one measure: it broke the shared fiction about Wall Street for all of us.

Much of the problem lies with the incentive system of Wall Street – financial rewards in return for growth. The system demands what too many companies can't provide.

Thriving is different than growing.

In this way, the whole system becomes untenable. Unless a new sector kicks off, there isn't enough mass in the early growth stages to counter the tremendous size and scale of those entering the late stages of growth decay.

And innovation can't save us, if it is innovation that simply replaces existing technology. To really grow the economy overall, we need what is called accretive innovation – new products and services in addition to those we have already – not just incremental innovation – replacements or improvements on what is there now.

We should not be surprised that business ethics are in decline when the 'valuation' beast has to be fed.

Alongside all this come the regular revelations about poor, unethical and corrupt business practice. It isn't as simple as a few bad actors; rather, it's the system that places such high demands on post-growth companies that bad acts become the only means to satisfy traders. Deceit becomes a desperate act for survival. As a result, bad becomes good when seen through the lens of efficiency as measured by survival and marketplace robustness. Desperately seeking to meet the expectations of stockholders and shareholders with growth by any means, corporations use ever more drastic, illusory measures to hide declining rates of growth. In the process they focus on ever more short-term thinking and short-term profits.

Trustworthiness is the very core of an economy.

The end result? Trust in the system itself collapses and decays as people realize how badly the system functions. This then undermines the wider social and political system as trust is at the root of effective financial and political action and transaction. This is a crucial lesson for the Great Unfolding – one we seem to have to learn again and again:

If you want an economy to thrive, build for trust. Make it worthy of trust. Reinforce the infrastructure to ensure good faith.

As the business universe seems set to implode, we face some catastrophic cascading impacts for a large number of people in the US and in the rest of the world. Are there options? Where is stability to be found in these changing times?

First of all, off Wall Street, small and medium size businesses don't necessarily face these issues. Many of them don't focus on infinite growth. For these companies, what matters is staying trim enough to be agile and robust enough to stay alive in lean times. While companies that are not publicly traded still focus on providing goods and services in profitable ways, the local mom-and-pop restaurant isn't trying to squeeze ever more tables into the room, ever more seats at every table, or ever more meals into every day (or whatever scaling innovations corporations create to prop up their rates of growth). They understand that there are natural limits – what Osenton calls the 'Theory of Natural Limits'. These companies suffer no illusions about infinitely increasing their sales. Small business isn't serving Wall Street stockholders and shareholders.

For the stockholder world to survive, companies past their growth peak will have to buy back their shares. Shares were designed to help emerging companies gather the investment they needed to grow. A useful mechanism. But if companies are not going to grow forever, we need processes and practices for shifting companies from the investment phase to the maturation phase. Or even into the hospice, if necessary. Right now the only acceptable way out for a business (or a nonprofit) is to be consumed by another as a prize catch. We need other options that can foster trust in the system as a whole.

An increasing demand for transparency, even in non-publicly traded companies, can ensure the work of the 'invisible hand.'

Non-publicly traded companies still account for a significant portion of the economy. These companies are primed to adapt to the changing business environment. Their profit margins may not allow their executives or owners to take multi-million dollar bonuses. But such bonuses only serve to magnify the extreme and increasing disparities between rich and poor. If you don't

think income 'diversity' is an issue for you, check the data from Richard
Wilkinson and if you want a glimpse into what emerging solutions to this
disparity might look like, explore the Slow Money movement, BALLE, and
all the Go-Local endeavors

More than this, a new sector is coming to life that makes more explicit a
method and measure for trustworthiness. B corporations, L3Cs, and other
For-Benefit Corporations, Social Enterprises, and blended models open
the way for a hybrid of business and social benefit. While this movement
has roots that are decades old, the scale and scope of the market is rapidly
expanding and offers an opportunity for our current form of capitalism to
evolve into one that pays more attention to the community it is part of, the
people it serves and employs, and the effects of all its actions and activities.
All this can help make it more trustworthy. Marketplaces for social business
expand daily, driven by companies that are still young enough to be in their
upward growth cycle and primed for investment. The returns are financial as
well as social/environmental.

The Political Reality

There is, of course, another disturbance beside the economic one – it
is the political disturbance described by Jane Mayer and others. It has
been brought about mostly because politics has morphed from being an
ideological to a corporate battleground as a result of campaign finance
'reform'.

Especially in the United States, what was once a useful distinction
between the left and the right has become the artificially crafted polarity
of two sides to the same position. As both the left and right have tried
to sway the margins of the opposing group, they have moved closer and
closer to the center. The political center becomes a gnarly knot. This is
the entanglement of the current political scene that serves funders (that is,
corporations) but means the left and right have come so close to the center
that they have collapsed into each other in a meaningless 'neo' muddle
where the seeming differences entrance voters while serving corporations
from both sides.

The interesting question becomes: Is there something else emerging?
Yes. And it isn't just the Tea Party. (Because parties that fight AGAINST
things rather than FOR things are not creative. They have no core once their
demands are met or become irrelevant – they implode without something

to fight against. This is yet another reason why the fear-mongering of the current Republican and Democratic parties is killing both sides.)

One way this emerging political movement is manifesting itself is as follows. On the left are Pragmatic Progressives focused on social justice, social change, and driven by a moral code based on equality. The Pragmatic Progressives may value justice over business, but they know business can be more just. They hope that their causes can become more resilient and financially self-stabilizing (rather than grant-dependent) by adding for-profit strategies. On the right, we find Libertarians emerging in place of Liberals. The Libertarians, valuing freedom, small government, and free markets want to show that we can 'bootstrap' ourselves and make it on our own – theirs is a vision of the rugged, autonomous individual. They feel that business – not government or philanthropy – is the solution to social ills.

Both sides show up together in a place called social enterprise. Attend events for social entrepreneurs, and you will see these people who, under the old model of politics, are at opposite ends of the spectrum, now rub shoulders, make deals, and agree vigorously on a path forward. What brings them together is the flag of individual agency – the idea that each of us has the right to act with agency in our lives.

Take a walk around Silicon Valley or across much of San Francisco. Peruse the funding models of Skoll, Omidyar, and other dot.com millionaires like Tim O'Reilly – a big advocate of Open Government. They are a strange blend of Stewart Brand's *Whole Earth Catalog* and self-made millionaire geeks. This is not a small group, and those in it wield significant financial and, more importantly, cultural influence.

Weave together the Pragmatic Progressives and the Libertarians (these outdated terms may soon be replaced). The old political poles of left and right disappear, and new poles of tension emerge. You will find a similar political 'crossover' or alignment at Slow Money and BALLE, for example.

Even more than that, this group – the Social Entrepreneur party, you might say – often closely aligns itself to another group – the Pirate Party or the Open Government/Transparency Party – which is emerging now in many parts of the world. Pirates are interested in shifting the way we handle intellectual property, strengthening individual privacy, and also increasing government transparency.

Identity was once constructed by what we bought or what party we belonged to. In the Great Unfolding, identity will be decided by what we make and whether others can share and build on that.

In the Great Unfolding, politics will continue to drive toward greater transparency. As people move away from the collapsed political center, it may be that the Unfolding brings with it a party focused on enabling agency at the individual and community level.

For now, the Great Unfolding is about the promise of the new systems we can step into as we move beyond the old polarized approach. The future is already here, it simply hasn't scaled nor been mapped yet. The edges move toward each other as the center collapses. It folds in upon itself. It unfolds a new era. The choice is between embracing this new era or trying to salvage a broken, limited past.

The Social Reality

Concurrent with the breakdowns in the financial and political space is a breakdown in the social space. A gap is emerging between two paradigms of social reality, which is mostly rooted in generational difference and the digital divide. Much has been said of the digital native. And we begin to see just how vast the breakdown is as people locked in the old era of social engagement fail to grasp – or even detect – the social aliveness of a new space. Twentieth century media companies survive on coach potatoes. Millions of them. When those people shift from passive participation to active creation and sharing, a different social reality emerges. Clay Shirky describes this in *Here Comes Everybody* and Don Tapscott covers it in *Wikinomics*.

This is not the surface froth of social media where everyone shares what they had for lunch. This is how Wikipedia got made; this is how news spreads faster on Twitter than on television; and this is how swarming hashtags tell us what is crystallizing in the collective mind of millions. The older generations bemoan the lack of leadership in the upcoming generations, blind to the consequences of a postmodern outlook that has toppled the image of the hero or leader.

New forms of social organization emerge with very different models of leadership and technology is piloting a new social order. Even now the meme is spreading to other industries where talk of "open sourcing this" and "open sourcing that" percolates through conversations where it was previously unheard.

The wiki-way of 'doing what you see needing to be done' instead of waiting for someone to tell you to do it means that anyone can be a leader.

Identity that was once based on status and wealth is increasingly based on merit – actions are more valuable than money. We shift from a world where what we each have announces our social position to one where what we have is shared – where relationship with others is what defines us. It matters less if I own it and more if I can have access when I need it through those I know and trust. I am what I share and who I share it with. I am not what I hoard to myself. I am what I do, right now and with others, not what I did in the past. As our society unfolds into a whole set of new values, priorities, and ways of being, those who can't see it are left behind wondering where everyone went.

The Social Unfolding is the most revolutionary of the four aspects we are looking at, as those who have stepped into the new era may hardly understand or recognize the older social order or its expectations. It is inherent in the wiki way and Buckminster Fuller's adage has never been truer: "You never change things by fighting the existing reality. To change something, build a new model that makes the existing model obsolete."

The Environmental Reality

Finally, the Environmental Unfolding, while perhaps less noticeable in some regards, forms the fourth aspect of the Great Unfolding. At first you may take me to mean that the environmental movement is gaining ground and that more people are aware of climate change. Sure, that unfolding seems obvious to most of us. But I mean something else.

Activists who have been fighting for sustainability and environmentalism since the 1970s and 80s have paved the way for some remarkable actions and progress toward greater awareness and engagement with the environment. Without them, we wouldn't talk about sustainability in any context, nor would we have so many of the current environmental regulations in place or wild places to enjoy. In some ways though it also feels like this movement has hit the limits to growth. What is happening?

A shift in awareness reveals an unfolding within the environmental movement too. People like me grew up recycling, growing our own food, being mindful of the environment. We were early to hear about – and respond to – the panic over climate change. Our childhood anxiety focused on the hole in the ozone layer. A few years – and in some cases decades – of panic about our environment has run us to an edge. We have had it. Enough. We can't get more people to sign a petition or change their business practices or eat more mindfully. So we have being doing some work on consciousness. Our own consciousness.

From that work, we become more free of judgments about others and find greater acceptance of ourselves and the world. The new unfolding story about the environmental movement is that mother nature isn't a weak and fragile baby we need to take care of. It is a powerful force to be worked with. Even established environmental nonprofits such as the Nature Conservancy have taken up the 'with' mode. It isn't about saving nature from us or saving nature for us, it is about working with our ecosystems to maintain them and improve quality of life for people too.

The shift is deep. It moves away from a self-righteousness that tended to offend those outside the movement. To make moral arguments about the environment only works for those who share those morals. Personal experience and clear incentives lay the groundwork for real transformation, regardless of moral philosophy.

Shaking fists doesn't win hearts for a long journey, but an inspiring and visionary story might. A story that is practical, grounded, and experience-based has a better chance than most of getting people to cross cultural and moral divides.

We need to shift from 'right vs wrong' action which creates 'us vs them' dynamics to pragmatic action with a 'what works here?' focus.

Because this evolution or unfolding in the environmental movement drops the antagonism generated by past activism, it becomes harder to see the size and shape of this collective. The people taking part in this unfolding don't necessarily resist capitalism or business. Their voices are not strident and antagonistic or media spectacular. It isn't about speeches and rallies. It is about being a work horse for purpose and vision. Being action-focused, these people, and I hope I am one of them, look at what is useful, what makes sense, and then whether it will make sense to others and be relevant to them.

Takeaway

What if this is the perfect storm? What if all the looming catastrophes turn out to be the 'near miss' that it takes to push humans to take a different view of each other and the world? What if a different world is unfolding right now. Different from the stories the media, our friends, our causes, our religions tell us.

It is not my intent to convince you that a different world is arriving. It is my intent to cast doubt on the current story, ripping an opening in it big enough to wonder what else might be possible. What adjacent possibility can we step into? If the dualist story that we have been living in turns out to be wrong – if there are many more options besides the simplistic left/right, good/bad choices we are offered – then what other strange attractors might be pulling on the fabric of our world?

While economic catastrophe and business failures hit the news and extend our sense of discomfort, there are also good businesses that can continue to be the backbone of our economy. They just aren't the media darlings on Wall Street. Trustworthiness is the core of exchange, which is, in turn, the basis of economic life. Where are we building more trust?

Politics is also imploding from a lack of trust, so the unfolding will champion transparency and bring together strange playmates who share goals around individual agency and the freedom to share information and ideas.

Our social reality is transforming too. The new form is imperceptible to those rooted in the old social order. "Do what you see needs doing!" might be the new motto. Power in this new social reality can be diffuse when it is attacked and can aggregate when it converges on a goal. If you haven't caught this cultural virus, then everything about it will probably confuse you.

Finally, the environmental reality unfolding has lost its self-righteous moral edge. This is giving it a new stealth, where environmentalists can be anywhere, calmly working to transform from where they are without raising fists or canvassing.

The 'us vs them' dynamic is faltering. There isn't a clear story of some 'other' that has been doing this to our world. We are the ones. The 'them' is simply all of 'us' together. So what are we going to do about ourselves? Can we show compassion for ourselves for our journey thus far and challenge ourselves to generate something more useful? What story can you imagine is unfolding? Welcome to thrivability and…

Level up!

CHAPTER 2

Stories

What story are you telling about your world? What story are you telling about your life?

We communicate meaning through stories. Stories help us locate ourselves. They tell us what is inside the story world and what is outside it. The sentences in a story form a topography of the space we occupy within the story – telling us the texture of the environment, where we are, and where we can go.

Stories can create a sense of empathy, connection, and relatedness.

Stories allow us to step into the lives and experiences of other people and inhabit other worlds from their point of view. Stories can also exclude, oppress, and undermine. They can do so explicitly through the action of the story or implicitly through the words chosen to describe.

Yes, this applies to the fiction you may enjoy reading for pleasure. And this applies to just about everything you perceive and think. You don't just stumble on the crack in the pavement, you tell a story about it. Or you already have a story about it. It isn't meaningful until you have a story about it. And once you have a story, that story can be so powerful that you may be willing to kill for it or die for it.

When you weave a story – especially a spiritual story – around a place, people may give meaning to their lives by acting on and for that story for hundreds of years. Consider Israel or Mecca! Different stories about a place can share the same facts but, by looking from different perspectives, they can construct discordant narratives.

Try it

$\top$ In the bravest moments in your life, what is the story that animated you?

- What about when you were most afraid?

- Did you ever have a change of heart? Did it have anything to do with a change in the story you believed at the time?

But this is not merely personal; it is cultural. Collectively we create stories to make sense of our world. What is the relationship between the United States and countries in Africa and the Middle East, South America and Southeast Asia? What story was the US telling about itself when it intervened in Korea, Vietnam and Chile in the mid 20th century? How had that story changed by the time it intervened in Iraq and Afghanistan in the early 21st century? And what has changed about the story as the US has contemplated engagement very differently in relation to Libya and Syria?

And this is also definitely at play in organizations – businesses, associations, schools, sports teams – where we can ask:

- What is the creation myth of our organization?

- What is the story that is told about our leadership?

- What story is told about how things get done around here?

There can still be a significant gap between the story being told about a business and what actually happens there. Nilofer Merchant refers to that gap as an 'Air Sandwich' which she describes as:

> "… a strategy that has clear vision and future direction on the top layer, day-to-day action on the bottom, and virtually nothing in the middle – no meaty key decisions that connect the two layers, no rich chewy center filling to align the new direction with new actions within the company."

In businesses, when the story that the management wants to have told about its work, products, and direction does not have credibility and follow-through from the organization's implementation teams, then we have conflicting stories. And those conflicting stories get subtly (and sometimes not so subtly) conveyed to the broader public. As parents we can leave a gap too, by saying what we believe in and value and then not consistently acting on it. We could say that integrity is the lack of a gap between the story we tell and the story we live out.

The stories we tell matter. They make meaning of our lives, our actions, our organizations. They bring us into alignment with one another. They fuel us to take action (or inhibit action).

Stories Create Action

Stories can stimulate emotion and thus catalyze action. I tell you a story about the neighbors where I heard the man yelling at the woman. She shrieked back. She sounded panicked to me. And then I heard a large thud as something hit the ground. I have not heard or seen from her in two days. I worry if she is okay. If I tell you that story, you may wonder why I didn't take action sooner. You may want to go and check for yourself. You may worry with me. But we are compelled to respond emotionally or physically to a story. As humans, we feel. And stories are one way we communicate with, and elicit feeling in, each other.

In marketing, businesses use stories to trigger our emotional wiring and compel action around their brands. If the story is successful, then you will identify with it and thus identify with the product, and become a consumer. Look at anything around you that has branding and you see the end result of story-telling through artwork, association, and emotion. This isn't just the old gimmick of a half-naked woman caressing a sports car.

When we buy products, we are buying the story behind those products.

In fact this is so powerful that we are willing to pay a higher price for an item that has a believable story for us or one we associate with. For example, we pay premium prices for brands we trust or brands associated with a lifestyle we aspire to. We buy the story.

These stories can get really complex and exist far beneath the surface of our everyday lives. Take aid to Africa, for example. Americans have a story about how Africa needs help. Never mind that it is not a country – it is a whole continent. Never mind that North Africa is culturally quite different from Sub-Saharan Africa. In the American cultural imagination there exists an Africa of starving black children, most of whom are dying from AIDS, few of whom have an education, and nearly all of whom live in corrupt regimes. In this cultural imagination, there is little room for the history of colonial exploitation and rule that Africans had to fight off. That has been erased from the story, or it is used to point to how 'new' and 'developing' the countries in Africa are.

And in this story, we Americans get to be the heroes. We get to come in with aid packages and tell people what to do. A current theme in this story is about how many Africans lack access to capital. Financial capital, of course. And implicitly we want them to be like us, in fact we pity them to the degree they are not like us. If we want to help them to be like us, they need to have access to capital so that they too can generate debt-based economies. We are so magnificent in this story of the cultural imagination that we believe we are helping them to become self-sufficient. And thus millions of dollars go into aid and into microfinance markets. We are exporting the idea of the free market. And only a few individuals raise their hands and say, "But sir, all due respect, is there another story we could tell?" Or, "Is the story we are telling one of respect and honoring rather than one that props up our collective ego and reinforces our sense of our own power?"

I was delivering my daughter in 2002, and my nurse was originally from Nigeria. She had such a happy way of moving about the room and being in conversation, even when she talked about her personal losses. I was struck by it. How different it was from engaging with someone from the US. She had such lightness about her. It wasn't the first time this perception had popped into my head, and it wouldn't be the last. In an age where our natural resources are diminishing and more and more of US culture radiates depression and sadness, why is it that so many African people (even when they come to places like the US) are happy? What are they doing right that we might learn from? What is that story?

A friend of mine recently shared a story about banker culture: "In a bank transaction, if you don't know who is getting screwed, then you're the one getting screwed." This comes from an old poker saying, "If you're in a poker game and don't know who the sucker is; the sucker is you." And a new meme runs along similar lines: "If you don't know what the product is, you're the product." A slightly modified parallel seems appropriate.

If you're not writing your own story, who is?

- What is the story you are telling about your world?
- What is the story you are telling about yourself?
- What other stories could you be telling?
- Which stories are most useful?

Try it

Draw three circles that touch but do not overlap. The first circle is for facts, the second is for your story, and the third is for alternative stories. Tell about an emotional event you experienced. Put the time or place of the story into the facts circle, add people who were present and any actions they took which were pertinent. Think like a detective here. What goes into your facts file? Any statements about how you feel, why it happened, what it means to you, who is to blame, and how it resolved go into the second circle (your story circle). Finally, in the third circle, create alternatives to any of the why, how, what statements from circle 2.

- Is it possible for the facts to stay the same and different stories be told about those facts?

- Which stories trigger your emotions?

- What different actions might you take based on the different stories?

Perspectives

Usually stories are told from a specific vantage point. Stories we read often have multiple viewpoints which generate the tension or humor of the story as they conflict and resolve. However, cultural stories often lack this multi-faceted approach.

We all too often operate from just a single perspective. Chimamanda Adichie artfully explains the danger of a single story. She says that a single story about Africa told by her peers at school – and even by her teachers – became so ingrained that she was seen as not being authentically African, even though she was in fact born and raised in Nigeria. She did not fit the story's (American) model of what an African is. She admits that she too has operated from a single story about other cultures as well.

By exposing ourselves to many stories – not just many story-tellers, but many different perspectives on the same facts – we create a multi-faceted view-finder on the world around us.

We can create hybrid or meta-stories that allow for the tensions between different perspectives. I would like to say it makes us more objective, but I think that takes it too far. We become less subjective and more inter-subjective, understanding the stories between stories, the stories underneath stories, the warp and weft of the fabric of our world.

Evolving Stories

As we acquire new information about the world, we may create or evolve our story about the world.

We have a tendency to take in only information that validates the story we already have about the world.

This tendency is most vividly on display in politics in the United States where two sides (there are other sides, but the dominant two sides) have a very different perspective on the world. (This isn't at odds with what I was saying earlier about the political parties. Although they BELIEVE very different things, because they are jostling for the center they tend to DO very similar things.) Both take in information, filtering it for what validates their perspective and story. To break out of this cycle of self-reinforcing beliefs, we have to step back to see a broader picture or accumulate evidence that forces us to confront our assumptions and perspective. Let us look at a few perspective-evolving ideas from the last decade.

With *The Tipping Point* Malcolm Gladwell captured a broad audience because he offered an explanation about how the world works – an explanation that was useful. It was more useful than the beliefs it supplanted. For example, we had previously understood change to be incremental – happening step by step by step. By identifying tipping points where one more small step leads to a major phase change (like the straw that broke the camel's back), he enabled us to grasp why certain things seemed to change very suddenly. Many of us began to include the idea of phase change in our stories about how the world can work.

Clay Shirky's *Here Comes Everybody* and *Cognitive Surplus* along with *Wikinomics* and a host of books on peer-to-peer activity and knowledge development also allow us to create or evolve new stories about how people can work together. Before these ideas entered the mainstream, we didn't have a story to explain why so many people would give so much time to collective endeavors that they were not paid for.

Challenging Breakdown Thinking

I challenged myself to create or evolve an alternative story to the following story, which I had heard over and over:

> *We seem to be living under the cloud of the apocalypse. Much reporting of global news focuses on the end of civilization as we know it, albeit in small steps. We are losing what we had and aren't moving into a better world (except in small isolated ways). AIDS and Bird Flu, genocide in Rwanda and violence in Sudan and Burma, nuclear proliferation, the Gulf Coast disaster 2.0 (with Katrina as 1.0), the Haiti earthquake and the tsunami in Japan (and so many other earthquakes, mud slides, volcanoes, and other weather/geological disasters) – plus economic crisis and climate change, the extinction of so many species, terrorism and the war on terror (which just grows fear and terror).*
>
> *On top of that comes overpopulation, sex slaves, child mortality issues, as well as deforestation, crumbling infrastructure...*
>
> *Confronting this situation, there are activists killing themselves with the martyr's dedication to changing things, couch potatoes in sedated near oblivion, and hedonistic wealth-seekers facing doom with greed and opulence. This is a story of crumbling and disintegration. Our globalized post-modern world tumbling through one catastrophe after another.*

I was and am tired of this story. I was tired of seeing faces worn down with the contraction of fear. I was weary of the negativity and desperation driving people to hate, divide, hoard, and fight. I was ready for some joy alongside the horror and suspense.

We victimize ourselves, and in that suffering, we victimize others with our trauma.

I don't want to fight for a world we already gave up on. So, what alternative story can we tell?

If you look for the flower emerging in the sidewalk – life pressing through without complaint or blame to assert its urge for sunlight, what do you see?

I am not suggesting that we deny the "brutal facts" as Jim Collins calls them. But I am saying that we all see those facts through a filter – through the lens of the story each of us is telling ourselves (and others) about the world. If we change the story, then we can see those facts in a fresh light – from a different vantage point.

Maybe it is also true that never before in human history have we known a greater wealth of possibility. This book is dedicated to the task of transforming our own stories of possibility.

Let us put aside our existing stories, sample the evidence, and create new stories that inspire, motivate, excite, and stimulate us with ideas about what we can co-create together.

What facts are we not including in our 'catastrophe story' that might be relevant to the creation of an alternative story? Here is a bullet point list to start with. Add your own additional points.

- Mortality rates in children under five have fallen by 50% since 1960. Another 45% could be saved with existing technology and additional will! That would knock child mortality rates down to just 5% of those we had in 1960!

- Peace is on the rise. Global conflict peaked in 1992 and has since been in a downward trend.

- In 1999, the United States EPA replaced the Pollution Standards Index (PSI) with the Air Quality Index (AQI) to incorporate new PM2.5 and Ozone standards. The effects of these laws have been very positive. In the United States between 1970 and 2006, citizens enjoyed the following reductions in annual pollution emissions:

  - carbon monoxide emissions fell from 197 million tons to 89 million tons

  - nitrogen oxide emissions fell from 27 million tons to 19 million tons

  - sulfur dioxide emissions fell from 31 million tons to 15 million tons

  - particulate emissions fell by 80%

  - lead emissions fell by more than 98%

Narratives of the Future

There are two basic – over-simplified – ways of grouping narratives about the future. Utopian and dystopian. Utopian visions offer the dreamy prospect of a future where all or most of our dilemmas resolve themselves, and we find a way to transcend our differences and live happily ever after. They draw us toward a vision of what we yearn for, but they often fail to take into account the full complexity of the issues, unintended consequences of addressing those issues, the full systemic interweaving, and human nature. As a result they paint unrealistic pictures of unachievable perfection.

If we take our best qualities to their logical extreme and imagine what that would look like – then we have a narrative of utopia. If, however, we take one or more of our worst qualities to the logical extreme and imagine what that looks like, we have a vision of dystopia. Dystopian visions allow us to test out what happens when some aspect or dimension of our culture remains unchecked. Think of books and movies like *1984, Brazil,* or *Blade Runner.* The whole genre of cyberpunk offers a warning about technology and corporatism running unchecked.

So what narratives currently animate us around the future?

Perhaps as a counter to cyberpunk, we have the idea of the 'Singularity'. With the incredible impact technology has had on culture, radically transforming how we live, work, and play together in the last century, some project the Singularity will arrive in the near future. The rates of technology growth and evolution, when tracked and then projected into the future, suggest we may hit a point where technology solves all our challenges, transports our awareness into cyberspace and prolongs life indefinitely. While this may feel like the Church of Technology predicting the second coming, there is a significant movement of people evolving these concepts and the tools they're using are worth watching.

Planetwork offers 'Metanature' as an alternative future. The narrative of Metanature, much like the future described as thriving, assumes that nature is leveling up and that we will attain a meta-stable state at a higher level of complexity where nature and technology co-evolve.

**Is there a future we can move toward that includes awareness of
the complexity of interlocking systems, individual agents coming
together to serve individual and collective needs, and where health
and opportunities increase?**

Transcending Old Stories

What new story could we be telling instead of this story of crisis and
catastrophe? Can we tell stories about thriving that ground themselves in the
facts of today's world?

Rather than just saying that the old story is wrong or that the facts on
which it's based are false, can we expand the story to include both the gritty
reality and the successes we are experiencing? That would create a more
realistic, multi-dimensional picture of our shared world.

I believe we need to find the dynamic tension in this multi-dimensional
picture and I invite and challenge you to create stories that navigate a
clear path between the polarity of optimism:pessimism. This ability to
transcend duality or polarity by living in the tensions of paradox is part of
the emergence we are undergoing now. For example, when we explore what
neuroscience is telling us about humans being wired to be empathic and
altruistic, it is not to say that humans are never greedy. It is to say that we
are not only greedy, we are also altruistic. And what you can expect from us
may vary depending on the conditions and context. In some situations, we
may value another person's life above our own. In other situations, we may
steal, cheat, and lie to get ahead. Individuals vary. And both descriptions are
accurate.

As we describe the alternative story to catastrophe thinking, it is not to
refute the past or the facts that lead and have led to catastrophe thinking; it
is to expand that perspective to include a broader view.

Stories That Inspire Greatness

When you think of great stories that inspire you or inspired others, what do
you think makes them great? What great things do you think humans have
done individually or collectively? And how were they possible? The further
back in history you look, the more likely it seems that great things were
achieved at the expense of a great number of people (usually slaves). For
example: the wonders of the ancient world. In the more recent past, there is
a greater sense of voluntary contribution.

The human spirit rises to collective action to do something that at the beginning seems unthinkable.

An example of this collective action would be the way the people of the United States came together during World War II. The United States as a whole radically altered its production and consumption of goods. Unemployment fell to its lowest point. The government rationed everything from tires to sugar, from footwear to jam. Victory Gardens were widely encouraged both in the US and abroad, creating greater resilience at a local level. Women went to work. And factories changed.

For a specific example, the Ford Motor Company had been making cars using an assembly line. This form of manufacturing was relatively new. The Roosevelt Administration asked the company to make planes instead. Eventually Ford's Willow Run plant would make 8,800 B-24s. Charles Sorensen, the VP of production, says:

> "Now, in one night, I was applying thirty-five years of production experience to planning the layout for building not only something I had never put together before, but the largest and most complicated of all air transport and in numbers and at a rate never before thought possible.

> Once again I was going on the principle I had enunciated many times at Ford: 'The only thing we can't make is something we can't think about.'"

Fifty years ago, in 1961, John F Kennedy inspired the nation by challenging us to go to the moon by the end of the decade. It was thought impossible at the time. While this was part of the cold war fight with Russia, it was also a vision for humanity. Kennedy said:

> "But this is not merely a race. Space is open to us now; and our eagerness to share its meaning is not governed by the efforts of others. We go into space because whatever mankind must undertake, free men must fully share."

The Human Condition

A vision for humanity that inspires great action always tells a story about how we will improve the human condition. Each parent wants a better life for their child, however that person defines it. And for most of human history, this has happened. Not perhaps in a single generation or even over several, but over many centuries, I believe the human condition improves as a whole. The idea of progress is intricately tied to the idea of improving the human condition – of our children specifically and all people in general.

But the story of that progress has been knocked down by the brutal facts of our immense success in the last 100 years. The truth is that our efforts to improve our world and our experience have been so successful that we are destroying that which we depend upon. And while this trajectory was clear to some in the early 1970s or before, it didn't reach wider awareness until very recently.

As I became aware of this, I found it incredibly depressing. Studying the facts I had gathered, I found myself gripped by fear – a fear that grew over the months and years. And then one day a mentor of mine, Arthur Brock, offered me a different story. That story has charged me with energy ever since. It is a simple one:

> *Nature, in the process of evolving, often consumes a massive amount of resources as it struggles to achieve the next evolutionary step. Could we look back, as a species, a hundred years from now, and say that all the consumption of natural resources and the damage to the environment was necessary, in fact critical, to our evolving?*

I believe that will only be possible if we imagine a future where it is true.

In the same way, we would not have made it to the moon unless we had imagined it and then committed ourselves to it. And we can't commit to a world of possibility if we focus only on what is breaking down, destroyed, lost, and damaged. We can only do that when we imagine improving the human condition, tell a story about what that can look like, and then apply the will, creativity, inspiration, and ability of the human collective. We need imagination, conviction, the willingness to commit resources, and we need the humility to work together. As Mihaly Csikszentmihalyi says:

> "...complexity consists of integration as well as differentiation. The task of the next decades and centuries is to realize this under-developed component of the mind. Just as we have learned to separate ourselves from each other and from the environment, we now need to learn how to reunite ourselves with other entities around us without losing our hard-won individuality. ...Recognizing

the limitations of human will, accepting a cooperative rather than a ruling role in the universe, we should feel the relief of the exile who is finally returning home."

We all know the words of Neil Armstrong, "That's one small step for man; one giant leap for mankind."

What giant leap are we willing to make? What greatness are we willing to aspire to... voluntarily and together?

Takeaway

Stories connect us. To each other, to ideas, to action. The stories we tell ourselves inspire us to take action. Who is writing your story for you? To write your own story, gather as many perspectives on the facts as you can find. Create your own multi-faceted viewfinder on the world. Take the initiative and evolve the stories you have. Most of us only take in new information if it fits our existing story. Look for ways you might expand your story so that it can include new information. So that it invites new information. Most of the stories I see in the world make someone the victim – usually ourselves. Changing the story to something else is not, however, about rejecting the gritty reality that is out there in our shared context. Changing the story is about casting doubt on the existing story and then seeking out new possibilities which can evolve the story.

Can you imagine a story of the future where man, machine, and nature interoperate harmoniously? Most of the stories we hear about the future have these three elements pitted against each other. What if, instead, they were mutually dependent, where the thriving of one was dependent on the thriving of the other two?

When we have risen to do great things together in the past, we aligned around a common story that inspired us. We have done the previously unimaginable together before. We went to the moon! A thrivable future is only going to be possible if we start by believing that it is indeed possible. It may take great effort or struggle. It will require us to give our best. But this is what we love about inspiring stories – they take courage to pursue. Do we have the courage to tell a story about thriving? The courage to take our existing stories and..

Level up!

CHAPTER 3

How to See a Very Big Picture

Before we explore more of the Great Unfolding and ways in which the world can thrive, I want to offer some tools to help us see our world clearly. For me to have caught a glimpse of the unfolding happening, I had to develop tools to shift my perspective and tell a different story than the ones I was being told – a different story than the one I was telling myself. Rather than ask you to buy the stories I am offering, I want to offer you the tools that I used to perceive the possibility of thriving. You decide for yourself what you perceive.

To develop a fuller story, we can look both more broadly and more deeply. Whether we are moving through a larger frame of time or space, zooming out to see a bigger picture enables us to produce a better map of the world we are telling a story about.

As a coach, when I am working with clients who feel stuck – especially if they feel emotional around a particular focus point – I invite 'zooming out' to see the context and a larger span of time. From there, we work to find a new and more useful perspective that allows other patterns to become visible.

In August of 2006, a friend and I drove from Chicago, Illinois to Half Moon Bay, California. We kayaked in Missouri, hiked the Grand Canyon, and walked in a petrified forest along the way. In the painted desert of Petrified Forest National Park, I marveled at the rocks that were once trees. I thought of all the years it took those huge trees to grow. And then for them to fall into a swamp and become rock. And for that rock to now be in the middle of a desert. My own life seemed so short in comparison. A batting of the eyelashes of time. In that moment, all my daily worries became of no consequence.

It is not nature that needs us. It is we that need nature.

I looked up to the stars. Time functions in the universe on a scale that the human mind struggles and fails, over and over again, to really comprehend. Looking at the stars, I realized how egocentric we are – worrying about 'our' environment. In the context of the universe, this blip in time is one experiment among zillions. We could destroy everything on our planet and the universe would continue on. There is something freeing about thinking of it this way. But this perspective isn't a license to destroy the planet and it demands that I take the responsibility to care for what is around me. No one else is going to care for what is around me – and what I depend on – as much as I am.

Zooming

We humans love to engage visually. Consider the magic Blue Marble moment. In December 1972, Apollo 17 captured an image of earth from 28,000 miles away and sent it home to us. It is one of the most widely distributed images in existence – the one where the blue oceans, land and clouds form a close up portrait of earth from space. Earth fills the frame.

It allows us to see ourselves at a scale unknown to us before. Everyone on earth is, in some sense, captured in that photo: we are all on this blue marble together in a background sea of dark space.

Then again, in a 1990 photo of Earth seen from about 3.7 billion miles, we appear as a tiny speck within the vast darkness of deep space. This is the image that Carl Sagan famously called the 'pale blue dot'. It is no longer a portrait of our fine planet, it becomes a landscape of space, where we are but a tiny element. We zoomed out so far as to be nearly immaterial.

And that distance is too great for us to engage with emotionally. We want to see ourselves in the center, the dominant object in the foreground – not because we think we are the center of the universe, but because we engage from where we are on tasks we feel are within our reach.

Just as my looking at the petrified rock may have made my life and my worries so small as to become meaningless, zooming out too far, while creating a sense of awe, can also result in a profound lack of agency and a feeling of being overwhelmed. Your favorite game designer would never design a game that made you feel that way! You wouldn't play the game.

To get new perspectives we can zoom in and out or move around the thing we want to see anew.

Just as we can change the stories that we tell ourselves about our world and our place in it, we can also choose the distance and magnification or telescoping that brings about a new frame. Imagine the photographer choosing the distance at which to engage the subject. Is it a portrait or a landscape? What else is contained in the frame? In our minds, we have the same ability to change what we have in the picture or viewfinder. Choose the frame that enables you to engage, to feel as if you have some agency in the outcome.

Context

We can also modify foreground and background or adjust the context of what we see. What if the blue marble image had been taken with the sun or moon in the background? Or Venus or Mars? Are we looking at two similar things or events and comparing them or at variations on the same possible event? When we adjust what we include in our frame of reference, we can radically change what we notice or how we feel. For example, in 2003, my partner and I bought a house. As I was placing furniture in the children's rooms, I was feeling thankful we had so much space compared to the previous house. Six months later, having engaged in conversation with social entrepreneurs in Uganda, I started thinking of the rooms as gigantic spaces large enough to house a whole family. My sense of abundance began to overwhelm me. The room had not changed size at all. Simply my view of it had changed because of what I was comparing it to. Consider the Müller-Lyer illusion. The lines are the same length, but they don't look like it.

Müller-Lyer illusion

We can also choose to work with knowledge of perceptual effects in our minds.

We can try to view situations from the imagined perspective of another person or thing. I was talking with a woman recently about what she thought 'enough' was for her. She said, "As long as I can't imagine my mother being offended by it." She had a very solid sense of her mother's frugality and what would offend her mother's sense of plentitude. While this might not help her convey to her financial advisor how much money she needed, she certainly had a clear question she could ask herself whenever she was buying anything: "Is this something that would offend my mother's sense of frugality?" Like the change of direction of the arrows on these lines (which changes our perception of their length), her mother's sense of frugality could shift perceptions of what is worth buying and what is too wasteful.

Cultivate Multiple Perspectives

In changing perspectives, I discourage fixating on a single perspective. Having several perspectives gives a more comprehensive and useful view.

Let's imagine we are working on an initiative that involves citizens, government, and businesses – for example, the use of a local commons such as water resources or fishing areas. Being able to step through the perspectives of each stakeholder can be immensely useful. It's easy enough to see from where you stand how others support – or detract from – what you want to achieve, but assuming positive intent on the part of others and imagining what they are trying to protect, offer, receive, and care for can be incredibly informative. I also encourage using a wild card perspective. What would an alien anthropologist see or notice?

Try changing perspective. What would it look like to your mentor… to your best friend… to a family member… to a stranger from halfway around the world? Do any of these distances or viewpoints give you a new way of seeing it or allow a different pattern to show up? If the situation involves a conflict with another person, describe the situation from your point of view, from theirs, and from that of a third party witness. I found this so helpful so often that I developed my own card game to play when I was stuck in one perspective or another. What would your cards, in your version of the game, include?

Use whatever works to dislocate the assumptions of a person, era, or culture.

I regularly use first, second, and third person perspectives, especially in resolving interpersonal conflicts. What is it that I (the person disturbed by the situation) see? If I really imagine what it is like to see from 'your' perspective, what do you see or notice? And what would a third (and neutral) party see or notice? I have even used this to understand different political opinions. It was hard to be angry with someone and oppose them vehemently when I really could see the world from their perspective and the positive intent they held. Once I understood this I became trans-partisan, because I could see how we need all these different perspectives in tension with each other to make our governments better.

In conflict resolution, it can be especially powerful to get all parties to step through each of these positions. This also works with different versions of ourselves through time. To do this, consider seeing from the perspective of 'my previous self, my present self, and a future self that has moved beyond this moment or decision.'

Time

Just as we moved in and out in respect to space, we can do the same with time. We can view time in several ways. Which of these viewpoints brings useful information to the situation at hand?

- From the past looking to the present: what would our ancestors have seen, said, or done? What would you have thought when you were ten? Or last year?

- In the present, as an accumulation of time in the past: how did we arrive here as a series of events and who is telling that story (one perspective or many)?

- Letting go of the past and focusing on the present: what is here before us in this moment released of any stories we have about the past (which may or may not be accurate)? This is particularly important when we have an opportunity to let go of blame (of ourselves or others).

- From the present into the future: what direction do I want this story to take?

- From the future to the present (or even the past): assuming that some desired future state has been reached, how would it have been possible to get there? In coaching, we call this future-pacing, and it can help us see fresh possibilities and patterns.

Time may pass at a constant rate, but our perception of it does not. Time clichés reveal this common experience: 'time flies' and 'a watched pot never boils' and so on. I remember watching from the doorway of the bathroom as my daughter slipped in the tub. Everything was in slow motion. Unfortunately my body was also stuck in slow motion. She chipped her front tooth, but in those few milliseconds of her fall I imagined far more serious injuries. All of my attention focused very narrowly in that time on processing her fall, calculating her trajectory, looking at the force of the moment and calculating the damage. It seemed to take forever! Have you had that experience of time dislocation?

Different cultures and places also have different experiences of time. Let's look at experience of duration first and then look at time perspectives.

Researchers investigating our perception of time can use simple methods like measuring how fast people walk or how long it takes at the post office to get a sense of how people in a given culture experience time duration. I have moved to a mid-sized town in Illinois from Chicago, and I regularly travel to New York, London and other fast-paced cities. At home, I move through the local grocery store at nearly twice the pace of fellow shoppers. Yet in New York I can get passed on the sidewalk. Grocery stores also know how irrational humans can be. They know that people are willing to shop for a half an hour, but if they have to wait more than five minutes for a cashier, many will abandon their carts and some will vow never to shop in the store again.

Our personal sense of agency in our experience of time is a hugely powerful driver. We may value agency (the ability to make a choice) over pragmatism (getting what we need).

Are our lives moving faster or slower? Are we getting busier? Many would argue that the internet has enabled us to lead faster and faster lives as we get faster and faster processing times for the things we do. How rare it is to talk to someone who isn't busy.

Will these faster processing times and our busyness enable a more thrivable world? I believe it is not our perception of the duration of time or our capacity to manage more projects faster that will enable a more thrivable world. Rather it will be the mindfulness to choose how we want to experience time. The awareness of how to modify our experience of time coupled with compassion for how others experience time give us a greater sense of autonomy and agency.

At the root of this experience of time, it is crucial to take back our sense of agency. It is not the device or technology that is making time go faster, it is our choice to engage in the stream of information and a willingness to be 'always on' that makes us slaves to our devices instead of our devices supporting our choices. We can institute boundaries. We don't need permission to do so.

We can be the subject – not the object – in a sentence about our engagement with technology.

Time, Focus, and Values

I just listed several ways of perceiving time. Professor Philip Zimbardo and colleagues talk about six broad categories that describe, sociologically, how we perceive time.

- Past Positive: we live in a state of happy reflection on what has happened already – nostalgia.

- Past Negative: we live in a state of unhappy reflection on what has happened already – regret.

- Present Hedonistic: we live in the moment for the pleasure it gives.

- Present Fated: we live with the deterministic view that our situation is dictated by a divine or supernatural force.

- Future Focus: we believe that hard work now is worthwhile because we will be rewarded in the future. (This approach depends on trust in the future.)

- Future Beyond Death: we believe that hard work in this lifetime will be rewarded after we die.

We are all born 'Present Hedonistic' and our upbringing and culture can shift us toward one of the others. Understanding our own preferences, and those of others, can reduce conflict and improve communication. For example, I often look at the climate change debate in this way, as well as the conflict my mother and I have about saving for retirement. She has confidence in a future where saving makes sense. I used to, but now I don't have that faith. So now I tend to be more present hedonistic than she is, at least around money. What are your time stances around burning issues? And those of the people you are in conflict with? Or in agreement with?

MindTime Technologies have a related methodology for understanding different psychological types. Their model is based on what time you focus your attention on:

- Future focus is rooted in hope. We envision possibility.

- ⊤ Past focus is rooted in the search for certainty. We learn from history, and act from what is known.

- ⊤ Present focus is rooted in the pursuit of continuity. This is helpful with planning and implementation from past action to tomorrow's goals.

I was sharing this with Benjamin Ellis of Redcatco. Benjamin has these dreamy soft eyes and boyish good looks, but behind that gentle face is a very keen and quick intelligence. We were at the Royal Festival Hall in London engaged in a rapid-fire, back and forth conversation when I shared about the different kinds of focus. It caught his attention and he laughed. I paraphrase him: Oh, yes, you can see each mindset in the layers of management. Generically, the C-level is about vision; middle management is about implementation and continuity; and the rest is about doing again what we know and trust will work based on past experience. The best leaders then convert visionary ideas into a story that is rooted in the experience of the past-focused members (and which they can feel confident in) and which offers a sense of continuity that middle managers can implement on.

Suddenly I could see what I had not seen before – that those of us who embrace the future and ideas of change are turning off the past-focused and sometimes the present-focused people if we don't have a good story to help them join us on the journey. No wonder change management is such a challenge.

Understanding what our own time preferences are helps us to know how to work with them. And more than that, we can learn how to cooperate with others who may have a different time-focus.

Being aware of other ways of perceiving time can improve communication and help navigate more effectively to achieve desired goals.

Try it

- ⊤ Use the triple approach of three perspectives when working on a problem or project.

- ⊤ What do we know from the past that can help us here? And what should we avoid doing again? (honor past-focus)

⊤   What vision can we aspire to that might lead us a to different result than we have had before? (honor future-focus)

⊤   How we will make the transition from where we are now to where we are going? (honor present-focus)

Compassion

One approach I use regularly for myself when driving is to imagine that another driver who is acting like a jerk is actually in a hurry because his mother is in hospital. He isn't being selfish and unreasonable; he is in emotional pain, filled with anxiety and urgency, and thus he deserves compassion. It is usually not true, I would guess, but the possibility that it might be true is enough to calm my nerves and irritation.

Or again, take any current issue and zoom out and around it. Place it under a metaphorical microscope. Describe it (either to someone else or by writing key information about it in a list). Look at it from a slightly greater distance... maybe from two feet? Or from down the street? What about from the treetops? What does it look like from an airplane?

Developing the ability to adjust our perspective and consciously choose a useful new perspective increases our sense of agency – our feeling that we can take action – in the world. By creating multiple ways of understanding what we are presented with and then choosing the view we want to hold, we create a much greater sense of agility and adaptability in ourselves. Furthermore, we increase our ability to experience compassion unclouded by our own perspectives and prejudices.

A thriving world is much more likely where there is greater compassion and personal adaptability.

The capacity to resolve conflicts peacefully can arise from these abilities as well. For the individual, this capacity can lead to a greater ease in the world and a higher likelihood of satisfaction and happiness.

However, there can also be side effects. We can perceive more suffering and feel a greater responsibility to others when we can experience compassion by exercising empathy with others. If we step into the experience of someone suffering, we can quickly be overcome with emotion as our compassion kicks in. At these times too, we may need to use these perspective-changing tools to balance the experience. When we can maintain our own balance (moderating but not suppressing our anger at injustice, say), we are more capable of taking action calmly and with clarity of purpose.

Much like learning to use a camera, it is not enough to know how to frame the view well. We must also learn how to adjust light and timing to improve the pictures we are taking so they work for us. When we create stories and perspectives that work for us as individuals and groups, we also become more capable of creating a world that works for us.

Try it

We can change the questions we ask to hit upon fresh ways of perceiving. For example, to remove some blinders we are wearing or assumptions we are operating from, try asking:

- why does this matter to me?

- how does this way of seeing serve me?

- how does seeing it this way allow movement for me?

- what does noticing this or taking this action get for me?

- what would I rather have, be, or do?

- what does this move me toward?

- what does it move me away from?

- what is behind my perceiving it this way?

- what evidence am I looking for?

- what evidence would change what I notice?

We can also consider how our values color our perspective and try to imagine what it would be like to hold different values, and what we would then notice.

Or imagine feeling differently about how things are. For example, if I am angry about how the government is taxing me, what would have to shift so I could feel grateful for paying taxes?

- List ten ways you receive benefit from things tax dollars pay for. (My own top three are roads, schools, and libraries.)

Takeaway

To tell new stories, it is useful to develop an ability to generate new perspectives. Shifting perspective can help give us insights into ourselves, others, and the world. You can shift the frame you have, zooming in or out, or adjusting the context of the story. You can learn how illusions trick us and then adjust for them. Use whatever works to dislocate existing assumptions about people, places, and culture. You can play games with yourself to create multiple perspectives on a situation.

Time plays a significant and yet often invisible role in our perspectives. Your sense of your ability to take action may be dependent on your relationship to time. How can you create more of a sense of your ability to act by making yourself the subject of your own sentences. Rather than saying "my tech took up my whole day," be the subject: "I decided to use the internet for three hours today." To continue developing your sense of your own agency, explore your own habits and preferences in the time perspectives you choose. And what directions can you move in to generate useful insights for yourself?

Strangely, all this perspective stuff expands our ability to be compassionate. If this is the only chapter that you read and it helps you to express more compassion, by stepping into other people's perspectives, I will be honored. A thriving world comes from this practiced ability to step into others' perspectives. Take your existing perspective and...

Level up!

CHAPTER 4

Interconnected Systems and Patterns

Let's try this perspective-shifting approach again. I invite you to zoom out with me. Way out. Out to the edges of the universe. Not to discover ourselves this time, but to discover the context we exist within. What is the shape of the universe? Do we even know? How do we establish its shape when we cannot get outside it to see it? Is it a foreground to some greater background? If it is, what difference does that make to us? How can we begin to be objective about something we are always and already inside?

We try to understand the world around us, when in fact we don't even know the shape of it. We can never become truly objective observers. And, as we've just seen, even if we can get outside some phenomenon, our perception is always already shaped by, and encoded within, a story we are telling. We are endlessly trapped within our culture and time.

So how do we expand what we know if we are always trapped within our culture and time?

One way to explain what we know is to use models. But the models will only work in a limited set of cases and will only offer probabilities. However, probability can help us form a reliable world view. For example, the 'brains-in-a-vat' problem asks – how do we know that we aren't just hooked up to some system that is triggering our nerves to have the experiences we seem to be having? How do we know we aren't living in the Matrix, for example? Laurence BonJour argues that we aren't brains-in-a-vat because of the improbability of our experience being generated with such consistency over such long spans of time. If we were brains-in-a-vat, we would expect to spot an abnormality somewhere at some point in time. We can't guarantee we are experiencing a real world rather than a crafted one, but the probability is so great, we should operate as if it is true.

What does the inclusion of probability in our story about the world and our understanding of it enable? Let's say we are climate scientists. How do we build a model that includes all of the complex and interacting factors (which we keep discovering there are more of)? We can't. To get anywhere at all, we have to use approximations and iterative thinking. We prototype, test, modify, and adapt. We talk about confidence levels.

A reductionist scientific approach focuses on creating models of how we think things work. We predict what is going to happen, and then we test those models to see if they work. If we get the results we expect, we call this proof that the model is accurate. However, over time we have discovered that these results may start to include sets of cases where they do not work.

Inevitably these anomalies undermine the models we had and lead to paradigm shifts in science and understanding. Thomas Kuhn, in *The Structure of Scientific Revolutions*, explains how paradigm shifts create more nuanced versions of our understanding that explain and model the world with increasing accuracy.

In a reductionist world, truth is obtainable. We can reduce the world to its component parts, create models of how these parts interact, and recreate the whole from the parts. This has been incredibly useful for us and produced some wonderful science. However, we now know that only a small subset of what we interact with functions in completely predictable ways.

As we continue to update paradigms, we begin to discover cases that don't fit into models because they change in unexpected ways!

Human beings, families, societies and ecosystems are all examples of complex adaptive systems. When we are dealing with complex adaptive systems, we find that models fail to give useful and consistent proof of their accuracy. The system loops back and adjusts itself based on the inputs it receives (that is to say, in response to what's happening 'out there'), and this self-organizing learning system can't be effectively modeled. We can't develop simple predictive frameworks. We can, however, use what we know to offer probabilities. And so our approach to evidence, experience and 'truth' evolves as the information we have evolves. We adapt. Some limited set of science can operate in a laboratory controlling for variables or generated from mathematical calculations, but the vast majority of science does not happen that way. We move away from grand theories to qualitative research on actual occurrences. Consider the atypical work of Elinor Ostrom, where she went into the field to observe. This is rare in economics.

In fact, we have this whole new field of behavioral economics opening up which is rooted in observing behavior.

We begin to see that our 'scientific' knowledge is evolving instead of being static. It expands and changes over time. Furthermore, it fails to predict accurately in a wide range of important situations.

If we can't predict and know the truth of why something happens, is there something useful we *can* know? Maybe we need not to hold on so tightly to the idea of an objective truth that will be known and true for all time. Instead, maybe we need what is useful to move us forward? Thus, the questions we ask can move away from 'why?' and toward 'how?' and the answers we get need only be better approximations and more useful iterations. As Steve Crandall, a physicist and inventor, would say, "we want our questions to lead to even better questions."

This is part of a much larger polarity swing between the world of theory and science and the ad hoc world of experience. We move toward a world of "what can I do with what we have?" – this shows up in wide ranging ways as Maker culture, asset-based community development, solutions-orientated thinking, and decision-theory in complex adaptive systems.

In asking 'how?', we don't presume that every way of seeing an occurrence will prompt the same answer.

We zoom in and out, move around and around, and interact. We play. We play until we find a perspective that captures a useful pattern. Let's playfully take a look at David Snowden's Cynefin framework to make a clearer distinction between what is useful to view through a reductionist lens and what is useful to view from a more organic perspective. Then we can explore a few of the key concepts of systems thinking that have been popularized in recent years and serve us well in understanding the context that we exist within.

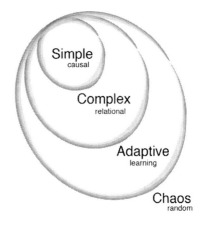

Simple
causal

Complex
relational

Adaptive
learning

Chaos
random

System Complexity Spectrum

Complexity, Complex Adaptive Systems, Chaos – and the Cynefin Framework

The last fifty years have brought about more refined understandings of complexity, systems, and chaos. Each responds to stimulus differently. Understanding these will help us grasp the current breakthroughs, how they can be transformative, and how to make decisions in different circumstances.

The Cynefin Framework helps us distinguish between simple, complicated, complex, and chaotic systems. If you're unfamiliar with this work, a summary and example may help.

Simple System – "I can model, therefore I can predict"

Here, the relationship between cause and effect is clear. Inputs and outputs are known. Snowden suggests that what we call 'best practices' fit simple systems. Here, what goes into the system directly affects what comes out. I put ingredients into a bowl and mix in the correct order. I bake for a dozen minutes, and then remove from the oven. I get cookies. They come out the same each time, as long as I am consistent about the temperature, quality and quantity and order of the ingredients, and the timing of each step. I can predict what will happen – the chocolate in the chocolate chip cookies will melt a little and the dough will dry and crisp some. They turn out best when I use butter. They burn less if I cook them on the right rack. We can write a list of what makes them work best. We might argue about what 'best' really means, but the process of making is very replicable. We can model how the cookies are made, then repeat, and we should get the same results. Yummy.

Complicated System – "If I analyze enough information, I can model and predict."

Here, the relationship between input and output isn't immediately obvious. It requires research and analysis. There are direct and indirect relationships with compounding factors. Here Snowden suggests we can apply 'good practice.'

Complicated systems differ from simple systems primarily in the amount of data we need to review in order to understand what is going inside and outside the system and how the parts interact. An example would be understanding how cookies get to the grocery store. It is not as obvious as making cookies at home. There is still a recipe but, instead of going to one store to get all the ingredients, a factory sources ingredients from many farmers and some might be shipped halfway around the world. The equipment in the factory may be much more complicated than the wooden spoon and bowl you use at home. And then the cookies get wrapped and packaged and shipped to stores to be sold. So when cookies are not on the shelf at the store where you expected them, it can take a lot more analysis to figure out what part of the system is not working properly. (Or we can just blame the shelving clerk, since he seems closest to the error we see.) There is a known and proper way for the system to work. And the outputs are predictable: cookies in boxes, ready to eat. Because of the scale of the system, it becomes harder to be sure our practices are the best possible practices. We can, with some confidence, say they are good. And we might discover something even better.

Complex Adaptive System – "Instead of looking for causality, I look for statistical relationships and patterns."

With Complex Adaptive Systems, even with analysis, the impacts of inputs can't be predicted. Effects create additional effects. Snowden encourages 'emergent practice' in complex adaptive situations.

Systems with a lot of interaction between interdependent nodes are called complex because the non-linear variations go beyond the scope of our mathematical tools: the sheer range and scope of their potential behavior prevents even large-scale computer analysis getting a glimpse of the possibilities. They show emergent behavior (behavior that cannot be predicted by studying its components) and surprisingly adaptive behavior when circumstances change. Markets, genetics, social interactions, even life itself may be a result of this adaptive complexity.

Using our cookie analogy, the cookie market is a complex system. Whose cookies are selling at what price in which stores? What happens in the market when we decrease the price, move the cookies in the aisle or shelf, or change the packaging? We may think we know, but we can't be sure. We take a risk and see what happens.

Complex Adaptive Systems, which are a specific case of complex systems, self-modify or exhibit adaptive learning. Imagine markets that learn that discount sales of cookies happen on weekends, so cookie sales decline during the week in anticipation of the weekend. Or maybe cookies adapt on their own. Maybe it is more mouth-watering to imagine cookies that learn to make themselves better. I want to open a box and have the cookies sense what kind I am hungry for and change into that flavor instead of having to choose for myself in the store.

Chaotic System – "I play with opportunities and disruptions."

Here, we find no known or comprehensible relationship between inputs and outputs. It seems random and completely unpredictable. For chaos, Snowden advises 'novel practice.'

Chaotic Systems, like complex systems, are not predictable. However, they are not-predictable to a much greater degree. The nonlinear dynamics of chaotic systems can mean that I put in the ingredients for cookies, and I get a mud house because the dough rose like bread to enormous proportions. Whatever I am uncertain about in terms of inputs can have such drastic compounding effects that any future prediction of output is made increasingly difficult. The Butterfly Effect is an instance of chaos – where small changes in the initial conditions can lead to drastically different results down the timeline. We will talk about compounding feedback loops and power laws which can create this amplification later.

Using the Cynefin framework helps us understand which narrative to use and thus which decision-making approach to apply. Are we in a chaotic environment trying to use best practices? The results will likely be disastrous and frustrating. Are we in a simple system and calling on small iterative responses? We may be moving way too cautiously!

While it might be nice to believe we live in a simple world that mechanistic reduction can explain, we don't. We live in an uncertain world filled – at least partially and perhaps critically – with complex interactions and self-organizing evolution.

I believe the most disastrous example of our failure to understand what kind of a world we live in is the way we humans have approached 'wicked problems' as if they were engineering challenges. Wicked problems are complex interdependent bundles of issues often with contradictory or changing requirements. There are no perfect solutions to these issues. You can't get 100%. You will not get an A on this exam. Improving one part of the issue leads to complications with another part. There are always unintended consequences!

For example, let's look back to the favored continent, Africa, and the lovely aid Americans like to give. Let's say the intervention you want to make is to work with farmers to grow food in hopes of reducing famine. Maybe you are even wildly successful helping farmers grow food. They try to sell it on an international market, and then you run into the hurdle of pricing and

US subsidies to our own farmers making it next to impossible for African farmers to sell any surplus they produce. Worse, while you were able to grow crops, the way you did it depleted the local water supply because you grew non-indigenous plants that needed more water than the area regularly gets. The consequences can cascade far beyond the original good intentions. And routinely do.

Solving the wicked problem of 'development' in Africa takes more than deep knowledge of farming, more than creativity in planting or even marketing. We also have to consider land ownership, climate, international policies, health (the family all came down with malaria this year and couldn't care for the fields), and more. In fact, so many interdependent elements come into play that no single person can explain their interactions or predict the impacts. The best we can do with wicked problems is emergent practice – which means we must constantly choose actions in response to what we are seeing now and unrelated to what we tried before. It means using rapid iteration and shared learning to try to mitigate the worst effects. If we are really, really lucky, we might happen on key leverage points, over time and with practice, to evolve how we address these wicked problems. This is also why efforts that have been tried and failed might still be useful at a different time. Be careful when someone warns you, 'we tried that' because even if it didn't work before, a complex adaptive or chaotic system might have changed so that it works now.

Useful Patterns

So we move from an age of reductionism – where we believed we could take things apart to understand them – to an age of emergence where we acknowledge that the whole is greater and more complex than the sum of the parts. And this awakening to emergence percolates its way through our cultural stories, bubbling up in many different areas of life. We put down the mechanistic metaphor that built factories, and we pick up the organic – and often fractal – metaphor of emergence to recognize – and in fact to catalyze – more complex and resilient ways of navigating the world. Sexy science these days describes emergent behavior. Search ngrams for terms like 'fractal', 'emergence', or 'adaptive'. Watch each uptick starting in the latter half of the twentieth century. Whereas words like 'mechanical' and 'factory' have been declining in use, with their peaks between the 1920s and 1950s.

Having said all that, reductionism is still useful to us. Like Newtonian Physics, it applies in many cases – just not in all cases. It applies in a specific subset of cases of our experience. And how do we navigate through the rest of our experience? What tools and ways of seeing are useful there? From Complexity Science to Network Theory, some useful patterns can help us see how our world works. In the following section, we will explore emergence, power laws, and phase changes. Then we explore metastable states before closing with System Health and ways to intervene in systems.

Emergence

Simply put, emergence is the way that complexity arises from simple elements and/or rules.

Perhaps you have noticed the rising popularity of ants in our cultural consciousness. And sometimes bees too! You probably also hear words like hive-behavior. What is it that is so magical about these creatures?

Emergence is one of the critical concepts that allows us to imagine that we are more than machines, that by coming together we create something greater than the sum of our parts.

Emergence is where magical-seeming properties arise from the coming together of components – properties that emerge not from the components themselves but from how those components interact with each other – birds in flight, for example. Of course, we could not predict from their anatomy that birds would exhibit flocking behavior. Taking apart their wings won't help us understand why or how they form flocks or how a flock can change direction without multiple collisions. Yet when we observe birds in flocks we can see that they follow simple rules that allow them to interact in a patterned way, which results in a collective organism that works.

Emergent behavior can be incredibly difficult to predict because the number of interactions among the components increases exponentially as the number of components increase. However, it is not just that the combination of components creates a significant number of possibilities, it is also that these possibilities create patterns. All life is coded by a small set of DNA molecules, with four bases which combine in a particular order and follow simple rules. The incredible variety of life is all based on the variety in the combinations of these four bases!

Power Laws

A slew of writers from Chris Anderson to Nassim Nicholas Taleb have explained the importance of power laws. Most of us grew up understanding bell curves (otherwise known as Gaussian distribution), where events tend to cluster around a particular mean. We were graded to fit them – a C being the average. Taleb calls the world of Gaussian distribution – where things tend toward the middle – Mediocristan. He gives the example of people at a stadium: their height, for example, tends toward an average height with some variety on either side. So far, so Gaussian. However, their income is not distributed in the same way. In our current world, income is distributed with a very few people (outliers) having extreme wealth and the vast majority having a fraction of that wealth, trailing off into a few with almost no money at all. This is a power law function, a feature of what Taleb calls Extremistan.

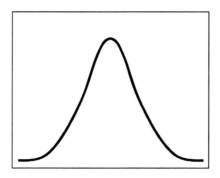 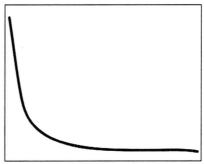

Bell (Gaussian) Curve   **Power Law, Long Tail**

Many things in our current world don't average out or fit a bell curve. Nor do Gaussian distributions explain or assist with outliers very well. It is not their function. And in a non-averaging world, using models that depend on averages can have disastrous results.

Malcolm Gladwell pointed out to us that we live in a world that celebrates outliers. How do we recognize them and account for them? The success of a book or an actor tends toward a power law – where a few do very well and the vast majority trickle off into a long tail. In the case of books, actors, and movies, these are essentially popularity contests in which those which become popular are more visible and thus become even more popular in self-reinforcing loops. These kinds of compounding effects create the exponential functions that produce power law statistics. In self-organizing systems, some feedback loops can be self-reinforcing, so the more of it we have, the more that gets created. We call these positive feedback loops. (Positive because they are self-reinforcing not because they necessarily have good outcomes.) Some scientists describe carbon emissions this way – the warmer it gets, the more arctic ice melts, revealing trapped methane in the tundra, leading to more carbon release, creating more warming, and so on... until the system reaches some breaking point – for example, all the methane is released.

Decision-Making

Decision-making in Extremistan is significantly different than it is in Mediocristan. Our ability to predict outcomes in Mediocristan is about taking a large enough sample and assuming that, in the vast majority of cases, we will get results near the middle. However, in Extremistan, average doesn't make sense. This may seem obvious, but we still make the mistake when telling stories about climate change or making predictions about the future of the environment.

Understanding power laws and the magic of the emerging long tail opportunities allows us to grasp a world in transformation that we could not have made sense of before. So we are learning how to anticipate our risks and find ways to manage them. We are learning how to assess our opportunities better. And we need to learn quickly now.

It is ever more pressing that we understand how to operate in Extremistan, as the consequences can be more radical than in Mediocristan. Taleb warns us that our assumptions about living in Mediocristan blind us to the rare and uncertain yet important events (such as discovering the existence of black swans at a time when everyone assumed all swans were white). While their probability might be incomputable, these are the events that mark our history and evolution. Kuhn also places these paradigm-shifting events in a special class: the class of rare events – of significant impact – that define a period or age. We can't see them coming or adequately account for them happening, but these outliers exist and the certainty with which we experience the uncertainty of their arrival may be one of our most important challenges.

This certainty about uncertainty does not mean that we must learn how to predict black swans. It means that we have to assume they will come, at some point, and that we have to create resilience in our systems for handling them when they do. More than just being able to survive these rare and massively significant events (which is resilience), we have to use them to become even better – what Taleb calls anti-fragile. Nietzsche might have said, "what doesn't kill us makes us stronger", but today we need to say, "I will actively learn to be stronger with every challenge."

We have to learn how to make useful decisions in a world where we are certain black swan events exist.

This is one of the crucial differences between resilient or sustainable approaches and thrivable ones. In the era of thrivability, we not only want to be survive challenges (sustainability) or adapt to challenges (resilience), we want to get better with each challenge. Bring it on! Like a hydra having her head cut off, we can grow two more in its place. Nature displays immense anti-fragile behavior. If you doubt it, look at the disturbing news about the growing resistance to antibiotics. Life is getting stronger because it was challenged. And we model from nature. How do we get stronger, not just in response to the usual vagaries of life, but also in response to the unexpected and potentially catastrophic challenge?

Try it:

‌   Draw a three column table.

‌   In the first column, list things that might be unexpected positive or negative events for you, your business, or your community.

‌   In the second column, list what you could do to prevent or encourage those events.

‌   In the third column, speculate what you could do so that you not only survive the negative events (or enjoy the positive ones) but actually become stronger/better/more able because of them.

Phase Shifts/Change

What Malcolm Gladwell popularized in *The Tipping Point* we can also call the point at which a phase shift occurs. In chemistry terms, we learn about changes in phases as water moves from being a liquid to being a solid or gas. And while it may take on different attributes depending on the temperature and speed at which the water freezes, it shifts from one phase to another without passing through a series of in-between incremental stages. This may seem obvious with the example of water, however we often expect change to be step-by-step, incremental when it isn't always the case.

There was probably a phase change in your life when you first bought a cell phone – or your first smart phone. However, as this change was probably not very painful to you, it didn't get logged in the mind as a phase change, despite the significant altering of your routines.

Some things do change incrementally. If the process is additive, such as building a house one beam and brick at a time, the change is incremental. However, in certain conditions, change may be exponential even when the process is additive. Let's say a disease spreads, as one person infects three to five others people. If each person in turn then infects three to five others, the rate of infection is going to be exponential. It soon reaches a point at which is becomes an epidemic. It isn't as if one less case makes it less of an epidemic. It is that it starts multiplying at a rate that turns it into an epidemic. And more and more aspects of our world take on this viral network effect as we see the same phenomenon in the spread of ideas, emotions, fashions, etc.

Let's digress for a moment to look at what qualities something needs to spread this way. An apple is a rival good. If I hand it to you, I can't then also hand it to someone else. In building a house, if I give you the beams and concrete, I can't give those same beams and concrete to someone else. Beams and concrete can't spread virally. Apple pips can take seed, grow into trees and bear fruit, but it takes generations for them to spread widely. But if I share my chocolate chip cookie recipe with you, I can also give it to five other friends in the same email. And they can each forward it to several of their friends. It is 'nonrival' goods, like the recipe, that can spread exponentially: ideas, disease, information – things that can be shared without reducing the number available for sharing. And as information flows accelerate and communication channels increase in size and number, more things can more easily spread virally.

When there is exponential change, we can collectively shift state very quickly.

Phase change struck me as vital when I was watching David P Reed talk about slime molds a few years ago. David is one of those computer scientist guys in their early sixties who played a role in the development of the internet (TCP/IP). He was schooled at MIT and is still there. He even has a 'law' of his own: "the utility of large networks, particularly social networks, can scale exponentially with the size of the network." He seems quiet at first glance, but if you ask a question about something he cares about, passion lights up his eyes, he leans forward and reveals his expansive knowledge and strong opinions. In this particular passionate expression, he was explaining how slime molds act as individual organisms under particular conditions. And if other conditions become present, the slime mold 'individuals' will aggregate into a collective slime mold. I find it hard to even fix singular and plural forms here, as the one-celled organism is seen as a single individual organism, but we also think of the collection of cells forming a slime mold organism.

Later I asked him to expound on it for, *Thrivability: A Collaborative Sketch*. He wrote:

> "...we wonder at the adaptability of a rather simple organism – the slime mold *Dictyostelium discoideum* – that thrives, depending on its environment, as a collection of single amoeba-like cells, a multi-celled mobile slug, and a plant-like stalk that disperses spores on the wind. Our bias towards seeing power as a centralized phenomenon led scientists to believe that certain mold cells must be the 'leaders' coordinating these actions, until Evelyn Fox Keller demonstrated that any cells can begin the processes that lead to transformation of shape and function, depending on conditions. Again we see that 'power at the edges' promotes surprising adaptability and evolvability, conferring a resilience upon the system."

Phase changes or transitions describe these small scale shifts between states. These changes from one state of relative stability to another can occur very quickly.

Metastability, a shift from one state to another relatively stable one, applies to whole systems.

The system exists in one state (able to endure some limited amount of disturbance and still return to a fairly steady system state) and then shifts to another state under certain conditions, where it can again be fairly stable.

It is very likely that you have experienced something like this metastable state-shifting repeatedly. Take the earlier example of buying your first smart phone. One day you didn't have one and you perhaps didn't particularly want one. And now you spend a significant portion of your time using it. That shift at the individual level was probably not very hard. But as enough people jumped in and got smart phones, the whole system evolved to another metastable state.

The shift from one metastable system state to another can appear to be operating like a power law if you zoom in 'too far', but from a broader view, the S-curves become clear, showing that the system has limits.

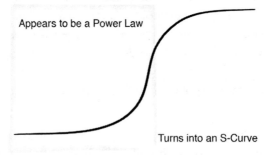

Appears to be a Power Law

Turns into an S-Curve

Power Law or S-Curve

In *Six Rules for Effective Forecasting*, Paul Saffo explains:

> "Change rarely unfolds in a straight line. The most important developments typically follow the S-curve shape of a power law: Change starts slowly and incrementally, putters along quietly, and then suddenly explodes, eventually tapering off and even dropping back down."

Jim Fournier's work at Planetwork offers one story that uses this model to describe the environmental and technological changes we are currently experiencing. What if we have collectively zoomed in 'too far' and are seeing the shape of a power law (with out world heading our of control toward catastrophe) when we are in fact in an S curve now, and nature will become enabled at a new metastable state? Metanature.

System Health and Intervention

There are at least two levels in a system. Making distinctions between these levels helps us understand system health. My great-aunt recently passed away and, around the same time, I saw pictures on Facebook of a newborn baby. At the level of the individuals involved, these are endings and beginnings. At the system level of humans in aggregate, this might be inflow and outflow in balance and signs that the system is holding fairly steady.

Flows

In a bathtub, if the rate of the water flowing in is less than the rate of the water flowing out, the amount of water in the tub will decrease. If the rate of the water flowing in is greater, the amount of water in the tub will increase (and possibly overflow). If we pay attention to a single drop of water, we may miss what is happening to the aggregate of water. If we focus on the whole system, we can lose track of what is happening for a single unit.

When I was a philosophy major, I tutored students in logic. I often found that students would read the content of the argument which then irritated some belief they held. So emotionally charged were their responses that they failed to see the structure of the argument (and whether the structure was flawed or not). We do this with systems too. We become emotionally attached to the instance and fail to see whether the structure is solid (or not) and how it is in flow. An example would be corporations focusing on quarterly earnings rather than the health of the ecosystem that supports them.

Can we hold both the health of the individual and the health of the system in our minds? Can we hold both the unit and the whole?

Let us look at the stories we tell. At an exhibit at the Field Museum in Chicago they mark six great extinctions on the floor as you move through millions of years of time. These are marked in red and signal a great stop in the creation of life. But where are the marks that indicate the proliferation of life where many new species emerged after each extinction?

Look one more layer up in the system (from individual to species and then from species to ecosystem). Ask: is the sum total of life creating more life? Is the bathtub of life filling up? And is that addition to life creating more possibility for life? As this bathtub of life fills up, does it overflow or damage the container holding it so that it can't continue to fill? Or does it allow the container it is in to evolve so it can hold an increasing amount of life? Is the increasing amount of life conducive to expanding potential? Or is there too much homophily – are the elements of the system becoming too similar – reducing the system's resilience.

We can do the same when we look at a corporate ecosystem. What matters most? Whether a particular company fails or whether the broader ecosystem of companies learns, grows, and evolves when a company fails? Within living systems, there will be decay and death. A thriving world is not one in which there is no death! It is one in which death serves a purpose for the whole.

A thriving world is one in which even death helps lead to the creation of more life at the highest layers of system health and evolution.

I was recently reading a fabulous work on systems thinking by Donella Meadows while staying at a farm in Northern California. It was quite fitting, as the cob hut I stayed in had a living roof and the sense of abundance and aliveness, even in winter, evoked a feeling of flourishing. Many years before, I had encountered *Dancing with Systems*. In this short work, she humbly describes how – after getting very frustrated with the way a group was trying to change a system – she walked to the white board and wrote down 12 ways to intervene in a system.

Meadows talks about systems as having stocks (the water in the tub, for example), inflows (water flowing in) and outflows (water flowing out). She says systems can have a purpose. And the purpose implies a goal (some state of inflow-outflow harmony).

The difference between current conditions and the goal is the discrepancy.

In the 12 points for intervening in systems, Meadows begins by observing that the things we intuitively choose to adjust – size of flows, containers, buffers, and time delays – are the hardest to change and give the least impact for the effort involved. Suppose a lake is polluted. Pollutants are dangerous when the amount of pollutant per gallon or liter is higher. To decrease the proportion of pollutant in the water, we might first argue that we need more water flowing through the system or larger bodies of water to disperse the pollutant. Making those changes would be time-consuming and difficult.

Next she points to filters and feedback loops in the system. These are often simpler to change and can have more impact. Negative feedback loops can slow down flows. For example, we can take daily measures of the pollution in the lake and prevent polluters from dumping water into the system on days when the system is over a threshold. Positive feedback loops speed up a process or increase a flow. For example, increasing oxygenation in the water can encourage healthy plants which can in turn increase the lake's ability to support fish. The fish droppings make better nourishment for plants, and thus a cycle of more plants and more fish is created (until some constraint is achieved). In human systems, this feedback can come in the form of information flows – either positive or negative.

Then Meadows points to the rules of the system and the ability to modify the system, or even the ability of the system to self-organize. For example, with traffic systems: How many cars can enter the road? How fast can they go? Can they change lanes or pass other cars? Rules can include incentives, punishments such as fines, and other constraints or encouragements.

Finally, Meadows tells us that the goals of the system and our ability to discern, develop, and adjust those goals can have a massive impact. Is the goal of health care to keep people from dying? Or is it to promote health and wellbeing? Those two different goals create different structures and priorities for health and our perception of success. Which leads to her two top points for intervention: changing the paradigm and providing the ability to evolve beyond the paradigm. In other words, we're talking about an intervention that helps to change the coherent set of beliefs and stories about how things work. Remember we began with perspective and with the stories that we tell?

The perspectives we hold and the stories that we tell have the greatest impact on what we take action on – how we engage with the systems that touch us.

Takeaway

In simple systems, simple models work and future events can be predicted. If only everything was so simple! Complicated or complex systems can be approached with sufficient computational power to be modeled and predicted. Thank the mathematicians and computer scientists! However, when we find complex adaptive systems, causality fails us. The best we can do is to look for statistical relationships and patterns. If you find yourself in a chaotic system, beware those positive feedback loops that can make any decision have exponential effects. Play with opportunities and disruptions.

Understanding that different systems (and systems within systems) have certain characteristics empowers us to make wiser decisions. Some changes are not incremental, they are total phase changes that shift the system to a new metastable state. Seek out patterns again. In simple systems, you can know what is happening. In complex adaptive systems, you can't. The rules of the game are different. Learn how to play this new game.

We push the boundaries of what we know ever outward. Learning to ask, "does this system learn over time?" helps you know whether you can expect it to change. It may not tell you how it will change, but you can see what makes it possible to change. As I say when facilitating open space, "Expect to be surprised!"

Ours is a very richly complex world of interoperating systems and interconnected complexities, filled with wicked messes. Developing tools to understand how these operate helps you navigate better, choose your actions more wisely and create better possibilities to come. You have to know, or at least make better guesses about, what to do, when, and how.

Look to nature. Nature makes use even of death, creating the compost for the new. In a thriving world, you too will turn everything you encounter into more value. Be anti-fragile.

When you intervene in systems, consider Donella Meadows work on interventions. The stories we tell and the goals we set can have far more powerful impact than the 'heavy-lifting' actions that we do day in and day out. Understand the systems we're involved in and...

Level up!

Summary of Part I

Some insights aren't pleasant experiences. Have you ever woken up and realized that the world doesn't work the way you thought it did? Moments like the assassination of John F. Kennedy and Martin Luther King or the events of 9/11 live in our collective memory in part because they trigger the uneasy realization that we live in world where those things are possible. We might much rather things could stay they way they were yesterday.

In this section on Perceiving I have suggested some tools that we can all use to get clear about our own viewpoints, prejudices and blinders – and about the stories that we tell ourselves and others. Tools that can give us a real sense of choice and of agency in our own lives. It's my experience that these tools can move us beyond personal or organizational resilience (the capacity to bounce back) to become anti-fragile (the capacity to bounce beyond) – even thrive – in the face of dramatic change.

I have tried to show that the myth of objectivity is cracking. The illusion that we can be objective is fading. But it doesn't mean that we have to be trapped in relativism. We are, however, caught irrevocably in our own time and culture, creating an intersubjective reality of our time. We evolve our understanding of the world together. We update our stories – our paradigms of how the world works. We encounter cases that don't fit into our story, and as Kuhn describes, we update our knowledge to include the new understandings of how the world operates with ever more discernment and nuance. Knowledge is not static. And our models and stories fail to accurately predict what comes next. Predictions are particularly challenging in complex adaptive situations with positive feedback loops.

I have invited you to look at the big picture, ask questions about what you see and what you want the world to be like. Acknowledge the current breakdowns as the negative feedback loops of an age we have passed beyond. Witness the current breakthroughs to the age we are emerging into. And tell a new story about what the present and the future can be. What possibilities can we step into?

I have invited you to consider where trust lives in our world and how we can foster more of it. I am clear about the need for us all to let go of the old us v them dynamic, because it is all 'us' now and we are all responsible for the state of the world we live in. 'We' are the new 'them.' Tell a different story about what you notice happening. Take action from these new stories. Cultivate your multi-faceted view finder on the world. Play games with yourself to create multiple perspectives on a situation. This ability to step into other perspectives generates compassion and empathy. Feel for others from their point of view. At the same time, recognize your own agency. Be the subject of your own sentences. You are not the victim of the system of the technology or nature. You are the subject of your own story.

Imagine a future where humans, machines, and nature cooperate harmoniously. It is only going to be possible if we start to imagine it. It is the moon trip of the current age!

The breakthroughs I describe in this book, I believe, lead to a phase transition – even a metastable state shift – for our culture. More than simply increasing our ability to adapt and evolve, I believe these changes in how we understand ourselves, measure ourselves, and take action can create new possibilities and allow new phenomena to emerge that are, just possibly, magnificent enough to counteract or transcend the breakdowns we hear so much about.

As we will find in the next chapter, creating thrivability is not about all of us converting, for example, to a way of perceiving that is future-focused. Becoming more thrivable requires simply that we recognize these different perspectives and recognize that they all have value to them. How can we translate between them? How can we better hear the concerns of past-focused colleagues, contributors, friends and family members? How can we better honor the drive for continuity in the present-focused? How can we hear the possibility of something better in the visionary, future-focused person? And how can we create teams and groups that include a useful mix of these perspectives when we have always tended to mix with people who focus on time the way we do?

Increasing our awareness about how systems operate and where to intervene in them unlocks more effective ways of interacting with the world around us and gives us agency – the capacity to contribute to making and shaping the way the world is.

And a brief nod to the materialists – I am talking here about ideas and stories using abstract graphing to make predictions. I am telling a story of possibility, not attempting to prove that something has happened.

PART II: UNDERSTANDING

Ever changed a belief? The moment when you realize all the evidence in favor of the world being flat was inadequate in the face of new evidence that the world is round? We often think belief change is hard, but it usually happens with the abrupt swiftness of a phase change. Yesterday we believed one thing, and today we believe something else.

Most recently, I had that belief change experience around vulnerability. After decades of trying to make myself invulnerable to the vagaries of life, I saw the famous Brené Brown Ted video on 'The Power of Vulnerability.' (She is another behavioralist, by the way.) I watched the talk repeatedly. Here was this forthright woman saying that, even while she resisted the results of her research, she had to conclude that wholehearted people embrace vulnerability. I come back, again and again, to the quote she uses in *Daring Greatly*:

> "It is not the critic who counts; not the man who points out how the strong man stumbles, or where the doer of deeds could have done them better. The credit belongs to the man who is actually in the arena, whose face is marred by dust and sweat and blood; who strives valiantly; who errs, who comes short again and again, because there is no effort without error and shortcoming; but who does actually strive to do the deeds; who knows great enthusiasms, the great devotions; who spends himself in a worthy cause; who at the best knows in the end the triumph of high achievement, and who at the worst, if he fails, at least fails while daring greatly."
> ~ US President Teddy Roosevelt

As the months passed, I could see how my own journey had led me from being cautious to being courageous. I could watch my beliefs peel away. Each time I watched it or read her books, I could feel another belief about what it means to be strong collapsing and reforming into a new belief about openness, anti-fragility, trust, and support. I could feel my need for control relaxing into a faith in my own ability to recover from whatever life brought me, as long as I was jumping into it with both feet. I am still struggling to value the 'players in the space' over the 'critics of their moves.' But I can at last see the value in shifting that view. I can stop being afraid of the critics, outside the ring, and focus my attention on being in the ring myself.

Back in 2004, when I was training to be an neuro-linguistics coach, we did a major section on belief change. My whole way of seeing the world had to shift to accommodate this ability to intentionally change what we believe. I experienced belief change first hand. I helped others do it. I got to see the inner workings of beliefs. One secret is that it's much easier to replace a belief with a different one than it is to just stop having one. We can trade in our beliefs for new ones, but we don't stop having them. We depend on them. Learning how fluid our beliefs can be, how easy it is to trade them in, can make holding any particular belief a bit challenging. At least it can be hard to take it very seriously. Maybe that is what made it easy for me to take on the new ways of understanding the world that I describe in Part II.

I challenge you to consider and shift some of your beliefs about how humans operate, how we come together, what we are doing in this emerging age, and how we can use information to support that shift. Come into the arena, here with me, to see what you need to know to create a thriving world for yourself. To uncover the story of thriving, let's dig into what we know about being human, our social world, and the data we gather about ourselves. Let's update and upgrade our beliefs. I will bring the evidence for the new beliefs if you will bring an openness to revising your beliefs.

CHAPTER 5

Irrational People Care

The cyborg anthropologist Amber Case says we often do as adults
something that relates to what we were fascinated by as nine-year-olds. (Can
you remember what you were enthralled with at that age?) It's true for me.

As a kid, I watched the PBS series, 'The Brain,' with fascination. I decided
I wanted to be a neurosurgeon. Over the last 20 years, I have been exploring
how brains work and how people think, learn, and behave through the
lenses of biology, philosophy, psychology, personal development, critical
theory, cultural theory, and the performance of identity. The last half dozen
years I have been following developments in neuroscience, behavioral
economics, and positive psychology. In this chapter, we will explore the
breakthroughs in these areas that make a thrivable world more possible
today.

Behavioral economics and positive psychology are two breakthroughs
that have radically altered our understanding of who we are as individuals
and how we interact together. They reveal that people, as a rule, care, that
they act from a place of empathy, and that we are all seeking meaning,
looking to make sense of what we encounter. They also reveal how
predictably irrational we are. While at first this may seem discouraging, it
doesn't have to be. When we recognize these assumptions and tendencies, it
makes a thrivable world more possible because we are no longer pretending
to be something we are not and we can stop designing our world for
that pretend version of us. It allows us to adjust our systems so that they
will nudge us toward the outcomes we consciously want. The increased
awareness of how irrational we are allows us to be more intentional about
how we do what we do.

This is not to say people can't be greedy or selfish or don't act from
self-interest. We do that too. But we *also* act altruistically and usually with
awareness of others and their feelings.

This recent shift in our understanding of how humans think and feel, make decisions, and create or innovate has deep implications for what is possible and what we can design to guide us into the kind of futures we want.

Refreshing our Models

So what is the story we tell about ourselves in a Darwinian world where capitalism is the dominant model for getting things done? First, it's generally accepted that the strongest – the fittest – will survive and prosper and the weakest will fall by the wayside unless they get government support. Second, traditional western economics, dating back to Adam Smith, describes humans as rational self-interested creatures. So we tend to assume that being kind to others is driven by selfish motives or, possibly, by enlightened self-interest.

For example: my neighbor comes over and asks for a cup of sugar so she can finish making the cookies she started. I loan it to her expecting that she will return the favor to me in the future. My self-interest is to create situations that ensure I will have what I need now and later, so I will be helpful to my neighbor to increase my own chance of 'survival' or success. Equally, I might loan it to her with the expectation that she will see me as a kind person and confirm my own idea of myself. (See Robert Cialdini's work on influence for an expanded list of these types of human wiring for social dynamics).

Two deep misunderstandings have encouraged these views. The first concerns Darwin and the second concerns Adam Smith. [Both arguments are well made elsewhere, I simply bring them to awareness here.]

First Darwin. The phrase 'survival of the fittest' gets bandied about a lot and applied out of context. Many people have used it to justify the idea that the strong should – and will – thrive and prosper and the weak should – and will – fail and die.

Fit is about having a place in an ecosystem.

From the bacteria living near deep underwater springs that are so hot they could boil a fish, to blind cave amphibians, humans, three-toed sloths, and kangaroos, the species that survive are the ones that fit well within their ecosystem. Not because they are strong or dominate other species. And not because any particular individual of the species excels, but because the species as a whole can effectively live and reproduce in its environment.

When we update this understanding of Darwin and the 'fittest,' we can stop valuing those who strong-arm their way to the top in social and business contexts. We can recognize where we fit, and how we can adjust to fit better in our ecosystem. We can value each part of an ecosystem for the fit it has. If we want to survive, we must find our fit. And thriving is about not only finding the place where we can survive, but the higher bar of finding the place where we can achieve wellbeing (and our wellbeing in its turn enables the wellbeing of everything around us). Thriving always includes interdependencies. We seek our fit, both on our planet and in our communities and businesses.

Try It

- ⊤ What, in your organization or community, seems the opposite of strong like a lion, and yet somehow fits and thrives?

- ⊤ What, in your organization or community, seems quite strong – like a lion – and yet seems on the verge of getting pushed out?

The second misunderstanding comes from several flaws in our understanding of Adam Smith. In his writing, Adam Smith argued for the free market and asserted its benefits to society at large. Likewise, he put forward the idea of an 'invisible hand' (suggesting that an individual industrialist pursuing his own unfettered self-interest will, unintentionally, act to benefit society at large). But Adam Smith also argued for regulation, although most libertarians won't point that out. All too often we slip from the idea that 'this is an element' to the idea that 'this is the only element' or from saying humans can be greedy to humans are only greedy. This is the root of the misunderstanding of Smith as well.

Smith was writing in a particular historical context – and he advocated improvements to the way that trade was happening then. However, he also expressed a great deal of concern over how communities would be cared for given that the motivations of business are not aligned with community needs. And thus he argued for regulations to ensure that business does not undermine the community or, in the terms we are using here, the ecosystem in which they exist.

I am not attempting here to fully convince you that Smith and Darwin are misunderstood, as that work has been done elsewhere. I hope that pointing it out here opens the possibility that something else might be possible, more accurate, and more useful. What might that be?

Human Wiring

Let's look at what science can tell us about how humans think, feel, and behave. Neuroscience has recently begun to reveal the mechanics of empathy and generosity (and many other phenomena as well). It turns out that humans are wired to be kind and that being helpful, being helped, or even witnessing someone being helped triggers what Jonathan Haidt calls feelings of 'elevation' which not only uplift us but can also be contagious.

The brain rewards us for being involved in helping regardless of what role we play: helper, helped, or witness.

This is not just enlightened self-interest, there is a pleasure in our brains from helping, being helped, or witnessing help. We evolved that way. Ancestors of ours who helped each other probably survived better than those who didn't.

Furthermore, neuroscience has suggested the existence of mirror neurons. These neurons respond to the visual data we generate from looking at another person's facial expression and create an internal experience of the emotional states that have generated that expression. You look across the dinner table at your partner's slight frown and furrowed brow. Your mirror neurons help you imagine yourself having the same slight frown and furrowed brow. Unconsciously you attempt to reproduce the emotional experience your partner is having. And often this is so potent that you will make a similar face in return. Because of these mirror neurons, emotions can be 'transferred' from one person to another.

I personally get delight from walking through downtown areas where people's faces hang heavy. Mischievously, I look them in the eye and smile at them. They can't help but smile back. Aha, I got you!

We are not standalone beings. We are not as disconnected from each other as we might have believed. Our chemistry rewards us for connection and kindness. When we recognize that our emotions are viruses that can spread to those around us, we can begin to take responsibility for our impact on the experience of those around us. Developing awareness about how our emotions spread to others (and how theirs spread to us) implies that we can learn to be more intentional about how we express our feelings. By understanding that we can be intentional with our feelings, we begin to take responsibility for the feelings we have. And we can learn how to design our environments and interpersonal dynamics to feed feelings of elevation for ourselves and others.

Alienating ourselves from others can lead to depression.

Choosing not to help others or not to see how often we help each other and only seeing the negative interactions between people leads to a depressing world – an unrealistic and depressing world. Our chemistry dictates that depression. Remember that you can decide what story you tell about the experience you are having?

Do you ever wonder why so many people give so much time to sharing and creating open source tools and knowledge? Yes to reputation. Yes to skills development. Yes to something about their sense of mastery. But without that sense of being helpful, they might give that time to other tasks that met those other needs better. Think about the last time you helped someone. How did you feel? And if they thanked you? How did that feel?

Try it

Reflect on the last 24 hours. Consider the interactions you had with other people in this short period. We can usually quickly name when people were not behaving cooperatively. But these stand out to us because the vast majority of interactions are positive experiences. List and describe the number of times that people were helpful. Challenge yourself to notice times of implicit or subtle cooperation as well times when someone lent you something or went out of their way to help. Consider:

- getting into an elevator
- other drivers on the road cooperating with the rules we agree to for the road
- people on the sidewalk, in hallways, and going through doors
- waiting in lines and clerks at counters
- people who smiled or otherwise pleasantly acknowledged you.

Connecting and helping is highly addictive. Our chemistry made sure of that. It is how a species as complex as ours survives.

If you think striving for a thrivable world will require too much of people, consider that we are wired to do it. Wired to help, be helped, and watch help: wired to feel with each other. We can make a choice. Be good to your brain – help someone. Even if you think the idea of a thrivable future is unachievable and prefer a take-pleasure-where-you-get-it approach... helping makes sense for you. Do it for the pure brain effect.

A smart hedonist is a helpful one.

Behavioral Economics

So we need to let go of the standard economic model of humans as rational actors. We are driven by much more than profit and self-interest. Dan Pink tells us that, while financial rewards may motivate better performance on mechanical tasks, they don't work for creative tasks. He asserts instead that humans strive for three things: mastery, autonomy, and purpose.

We are driven by our desire to be autonomous, masters of our work, and full of purpose.

We like to do things for a reason we believe in. We like to get better and better at things we do, and we want to be self-directed. If we know this about ourselves and others, what will that enable us to do now that we could not do before?

We are beginning to understand – from testing in practice instead of grand theories of the mind – how humans operate. We are learning how to design a world that works for how we actually are. While we may not be as rational as we might have liked to think, our irrationality is at least predictable. There are mechanisms of the brain that can be relied on to operate in specific ways. We can then take this learning and apply it to shift unhealthy behaviors, select better defaults, encourage appropriate behaviors, and influence culture. This can be about something a simple as pricing or as complex as a lifestyle.

For example, as you motor up Lake Shore Drive in Chicago you might notice that there are white lines across the pavement on the big curve on the north side of Streeterville. Say hello to behavioral economics in practice. The lines on the pavement make you feel as if you are going faster than you are. So, you are more likely to slow down. They work more subtly and yet more effectively than speed reduction signs.

Or imagine you were designing a contest to crowdsource useful apps for gathering and displaying city data? Keep in mind that money isn't a good reward for creativity. Put enough in the pot to get people to take action, offer a shared purpose, acknowledge mastery when you see it, then stand back and let the creativity flow. Let the real prize be participants' own delight in the work they're doing and wide recognition of the way that they are helping other citizens.

Working in a corporation? Give acknowledgment and reputation tokens to creative individuals and teams. Save bonuses for linear task work and group success metrics.

Which brings us to the dark side of behavioral economics. Like it or not, we become manipulators – changing the world around us by using our understanding of how people work. If advertising can be insidious, the risk with behavioral economics is greater. Who gets to choose what the defaults in a system are? Who benefits from that default (which most people will select without using slow thinking)? Well, first we have to acknowledge that this manipulation is always already happening. We are persuaded, encouraged, inclined to spend our money, our evenings, our weekends, our time at work the way we do by what others say, by how much money we have, by what sounds like it will be fun or rewarding, and so on. There is no place where we aren't influenced by our culture, our surroundings, and those around us. Second, all we can do is to bring critical awareness to these behavioral economic or neuro-scientific ideas and applications. We can't pretend not to be manipulative. But we can keep an eye on ourselves and others, questioning who benefits from any manipulation and where we will drop our guard and let the designs of other humans direct our course of action. Transparency in the way these decisions are made is an essential safeguard. And, if people are not greedy and rational all the time, then some of these system designers will be looking out for us, at least some of the time.

Iain McGilchrist describes the consequences of linear, 'rational actor' thinking on the world in his book, *The Master and His Emissary*. Jonathan Haidt, in *The Righteous Mind* distinguishes between the rider and the elephant, with the rider being the rational conscious mind. Daniel Kahneman, the father of behavioral economics, reveals in *Thinking, Fast and Slow* that so much of what we do is fast thinking based on our biases and clumsy heuristics rather than careful, rational, slow thinking. All three are pointing to our having this small conscious mind with a giant unconscious mind behind it. Understanding this better, as we are learning to do, helps us to design the world for more thriving. We can also learn when to trigger which domains of the mind and what to expect better from each. This and other work in the last decade or so on behavioral economics and neuroscience points to another unfolding. We are starting to move from left/right brain stories – ones that play creativity against rationality – toward what I call front/back stories where the attention is on the conscious vs. the 'automatic' or unconscious.

As we learn about the human brain, we discover that large parts of it don't operate like a computer at all. It is a complex and dynamic system, only a small portion of which is the conscious mind. In bringing our full minds to the making of a thrivable world, we bring in the vast unknown wisdom of the brain:

- The ability to connect disparate pieces of data into interesting groups with lightning speed

- The ability to hold opposing thoughts simultaneously

- And the brain tickles we get from play.

Becoming clear about just how unconscious we are most of the time and how rarely that 'rational actor' appears, we can shift our expectations of ourselves and others. If we begin to design for our whole minds as they are, what systems and culture could we then create?

Behavioral economics can transform how we design our exterior world. A thrivable world can result from using motivation mechanisms to 'gamify' the tasks we need to accomplish as individuals and groups. We can be nudged toward healthy behaviors. We can be swayed (although this is often not an issue of logic – decisions are emotional in nature.) One of the key drivers here is play.

A thrivable world has got to have play!

The 'rational actor' seemed to have little room for play and laughter. And yet, we learn in innovation and creativity research that play is crucial for creativity! And it is so much more fun that way too. Who wants a world without fun? Just getting by? Barely surviving? Where is a vision of a future that is healthy, alive, vibrant, and playful? Let's make that together. There's lots more on all this in Chapter 10 but, for now, get happy and…

Level up!

Let's use our awareness of how we work to make our world work better.

Positive Psychology

After ages of focusing on illness, psychology has refocused (at least in part) on positive psychology (the scientific study of human flourishing). Recent research reveals more about altruism, the compassionate instinct, and authentic happiness. In fact, Jonathan Haidt says we are 'Wired to be Inspired.'

One of the most head-turning things I learned in my early exploration of positive psychology is that people who can cover their basic needs are roughly as happy as people of great wealth. In fact it makes little difference to how happy you are, where you are financially – provided you're not in poverty. What difference it does make quickly diminishes as wealth increases.

More than that, giving away money has been shown to produce more pleasure in the brain than spending it!

Happiness turns out to be highly relative too, so mostly you just compare if you are happier today than yesterday. In his book, *Satisfaction*, Gregory Berns shares a study that showed lottery winners and paraplegics are equally happy one year after the event. When I read it the first time, I am sure my chin nearly hit the floor as my understanding of happiness had to adjust to this new data.

Positive psychology and the psychology of happiness troubles me still. Much of the research being done in this space changes what we know about ourselves in powerful ways that excite me. However, uptake of that research into the culture at large needs refinement. Too often the research is used to justify the exclusion of 'gritty reality' and the glorification of blind positivity.

Also happiness seems to be over-rated, if we listen to Berns. Wellbeing and satisfaction seem like better descriptions of what we need and should be looking for. Some people are talking more about *eudaimonia*, which translates as 'human flourishing' or, dare I say, 'thriving'!

The father of positive psychology, Martin Seligman, offers clarification of the kinds of happiness. There is, of course, happiness from hedonistic pleasure. However, he warns us that we quickly get used to that one. It palls. How often do you enjoy your fourth or fifth bite of dessert? You get used to the taste and move on, even if you go through the motions and finish eating it. Then he talks about the happiness of 'flow' states, which I will cover later in this chapter. And thirdly, he describes the happiness of being 'on purpose.' This third happiness does not look like a smiley face. It looks more like the satisfaction of knowing you are doing what you want to be doing for reasons that you believe in. A thriving, flourishing world, I believe, has more people with this third form of happiness. The joy of purpose.

Positive Intent

I first started exploring positive psychology when I was training as a neuro-linguistics coach. One of the core assumptions of the practice was that people act from positive intent. Another basic assumption was that people do the best they can with what they have at the time. These really seemed to name a truth about my own life and choices as well as make sense of the world around me. So much of what I perceived about the world shifted very quickly as I saw personal slights or even crime from a new vantage point: positive intent.

What if, instead of paying attention to the outcome or the cost to me of these things, I look behind that to what the other person is trying to achieve through their actions. And instead of judging them for not choosing differently, what if I give them the benefit of the doubt and accept that they are choosing as best they can with what they know, feel, and have?

Compassion for other people poured into me. Instead of wanting to punish people or avoid them, I felt drawn to find a way that I could create more options for people to choose from. I wanted to help create more awareness of the options that would honor their highest and best intentions. Next time you experience conflict, ask yourself, "what is the positive intention here?" In the roughly ten years since I have shifted to this way of seeing the world and other people's actions, I have noticed how it reduced conflict, anger, and resentment in my life. Rather than getting trapped in stories of how cruel or selfish humans can be, I shift quickly to wondering how I can be helpful. It is easier to find generative ways of engaging with 'destructive' behaviors.

When we stop viewing other humans as malicious, vindictive, and cruel, and instead view them as vulnerable, struggling, and challenged; we get a different conversation. And a different outcome. Level up!

Predictors

Another key insight that surprised me in exploring how the brain/mind works was how bad we are at predicting as well as remembering our experience.

Healthy, wholehearted humans can, and do, convince ourselves that just about anything that happens to us is good for us.

You may think losing your job is a terrible thing before it happens. And it might feel bad when it does (but not as terrible as you thought). And two years later you might look back thankful that it happened because it triggered you to actually start that business you always wanted to have. Not everyone does this, but resilient (or anti-fragile if we remember back to Nicholas Taleb in Chapter 4) and healthy people do it all the time. Brené Brown expresses her surprise, in her social research on shame and vulnerability, that wholehearted people have as much conflict as everyone else in their lives; she explains that the essential difference is the way they expect that conflict, allow for it, and believe they can make it through.

Try It

╤   List five events in your life that had a strong emotional component.

╤   Under each item, describe how you felt before the event. Where you excited? Anxious? Fearful? Maybe all of the above?

╤   Then describe how you felt during the event. How was it going for you during the minutes, hours, or days of the event?

╤   Finally, describe how you felt after the event. Shortly after? And months later? How about now, looking back?

We make so many decisions by using predictions about how much happiness they will bring us (or, at least, how far they will help us avoid pain). Maybe we can make better decisions about those things if we understand just how resilient we can be in the face of whatever outcomes our choice brings.

This seems especially clear when we have to 'give up' things in 'sacrifice mode' in order to live more sustainably. We think of them as sacrifices – and yet, many who make these changes report being happier afterwards.

One study of car-loving people who agreed to give up their car temporarily and use a car-sharing service found that many (100 out of the 250 participants in 2009) opted to remain without their cars afterwards. Zipcar now does annual Low Car Diets to continue the experiment.

Think twice about what will make you or the people around you happy.

I went canoeing with my kids. We camped each night on the shores of the river. One night, the usually brilliantly starlit sky hung heavy with clouds. As we slept, lightning and thunder symphonies began. The next day, the kids curled up under a tarp in the bow of the canoe, hiding from the pouring rain as I paddled down river. I sat in the back laughing and delighted (though I would have probably preferred a warm sunny day, perfect for swimming if you had asked me beforehand). I knew from my memories of my outdoor adventures in the past that these crazy moments are the ones I cherish the most. I want to be in touch with nature as she is, far away from solid roofs, air conditioning, and climate-controlled cars. So I delighted in knowing that, in the future, I would look back and deeply cherish this paddle through the pouring rain. And indeed I have.

So many beliefs about happiness turn out to be culturally constructed myths. They turn out to be wrong.

Happiness is perhaps an area we should get more rational about.

Look at the data. Reflect on your own life. When were you happy? Start a diary. Record your sense of happiness about an event on the day it happens, a week later, and a year later. How does your perception change?

Learning this has triggered a huge sense of ease in my own practices. I recently got a new car. My partner was helping me make a decision. We went over all the data with each other repeatedly. I settled on two options. I went to one dealer, who didn't have the car I wanted. I went to the other dealer and bought the other kind of car. My partner couldn't believe I could be so lighthearted about such a major purchase. I replied that both were very good rational choices – hardly distinguishable. I would be satisfied with either option, and whatever I came home with I would later say I was lucky to have. So I wanted the immediate gratification of driving home in one of the two cars I had finally chosen. So I just went with it. Making sure I got what I wanted from a car was much earlier in the decision-making process. Why churn? Why get tangled making a decision when I will be happy either way? Would I have made the decision this way a decade ago? No. It is because I learned to trust myself to be happy with the choice in hindsight – having done so much research on positive intent, positive psychology, and prediction – that I can be light about the decision between the final two cars.

As we learn about how happiness works in humans, we can get better at describing changes we need to make in terms of the emotional benefits they provide, so we can guide people away from the 'sacrifice' mode which focuses on what we are losing or giving up. As we come to understand more about how humans' brains work, we can change the stories we tell ourselves and others about what is happening, about the decisions and choices we are making, and about the predictions we have for what will happen as a result of those decisions and choices. We come to a better understanding of the rules of the 'Being Human' game.

The thriving world we create will be fun and exciting, drawing us toward it. We will get there because it appeals to us, and we know how to design for being human.

Meaning and Flow

Humans are deeply driven to create meaning. Meaning is the sense we make of life and the events we experience within it. What is it all for? What is my life for? Some of us reflect deeply on this and look for our own answers, while others opt for tried-and-tested philosophical or spiritual structures, but all of us have a way of making meaning in our lives.

Surprisingly, it is often the crises and seeming catastrophes that give our lives meaning. What about:

∓ the cancer survivor who creates a nonprofit to help others who have a similar experience?

∓ the disabled person who does something no one thought possible given the disability?

∓ the mother of a dead soldier who starts a peace movement?

These days, we also understand more about the conditions we need for productive and joyful work or flow experiences from Mihaly Csikszentmihalyi. He explains that it is not about having an easy or luxurious life:

> "Subjective experience is not just one of the dimensions of life, it is life itself. Material conditions are secondary: they only affect us indirectly, by way of experience. Flow, and even pleasure, on the other hand benefit the quality of life directly. Health, money, and other material advantages may or may not improve life. Unless a person has learned to control psychic energy, chances are such advantages will be useless."

When we applaud inspirational people, what we are cheering is the drive of the human spirit to make meaning out of the pain of our existence and transform it into action.

We often find people inspirational because they have taken their worst moment and decided it was a calling to dedicate every ounce of themselves to doing something to transform it. They take the meaning that is a cultural given – 'this moment is trauma' – and remake it into 'this moment is triumph.'

Summarizing studies at the University of Milan, Csikszentmihalyi says, "The reason tragic events were seen as positive was that they presented the victim with very clear goals while reducing the contradictory and inessential choices." What might we learn from these survivors? Might they be an inspiration to us as thrivers – those that overcome adversity? He goes on to say,

> "Flow drives individuals to creativity and outstanding achievement. The necessity to develop increasingly refined skills to sustain enjoyment is what lies behind the evolution of culture. It motivates both individuals and cultures to change into more complex entities. The rewards of creating order in experience provide the energy that propels evolution – they pave the way for those dimly imagined descendants of ours, more complex and wise than we are, who will soon take our place."

Yes, it is not sufficient to evolve our understanding of biology, math, art, organizational development, behavior, knowledge management, or any other field without the larger context of why that matters. Csikszentmihalyi says:

> "…to change all existence into a flow experience, it is not sufficient to learn merely how to control moment-by-moment states of consciousness. It is also necessary to have an overall context of goals for the events of everyday life to make sense."

As a society, we can choose to face our challenges the way the inspirational people we admire do. We can take the tragic events we experience, individually and collectively, and use them to clarify our goals. When we create a context for those goals to make sense for us as a society and through our everyday actions, I am profoundly convinced that the world we will create will thrive more and more over time.

What happens when we take the current stories of catastrophe and use them to refine our goals? What if we use them to move beyond our current incentives (GDP, individual wealth, etc.) and clarify that the positive intent behind those goals was really to achieve wellbeing for ourselves and those we care about? When we change our goals (one of Donella Meadows' preferred intervention points in a system) we shift the system itself. What might be possible if the understanding of how humans' minds work, as described here, influences policy decisions, organizational strategy, and personal choices? How might that cascade through a million small decisions operating from a different story about possibility, to create a phase change in our culture toward a more thriving world for each and all of us. A world that can work better for us, as we are?

Multiple Intelligences

Can we do it? Are we smart enough to reach for a thrivable world or are all the smart people working on Wall Street? For a century or more, IQ (Intelligence Quotient) has been a primary measure of a person's potential. However, it has been shown that high IQ produces neither happiness nor success. Howard Gardner, Dan Goleman and others have shown that emotional intelligence and other ways of knowing and understanding also influence an individual's potential. Recently scientists have shown that brain cells are not only located in the head, but this tissue is also present in the heart, the gut, and other areas of the body.

Stop and be with that for a minute. Your gut reaction is really a trigger from nerves in your gut. Your brain is not just in your head.

What happens when you awaken your whole body to being aware and perceptive?

To have a high IQ is not enough in the face of the breakdowns the world faces, and many people with high IQs have acknowledged that. It looks as if we need the full spectrum of intelligence, including emotional intelligence, to transform our society into one that is more clearly thriving. We need contextual intelligence to appreciate the ecosystems we participate in. We need somatic intelligence to listen to what our bodies know (including those distributed brains). We need creative intelligence to dream new possibilities. We need all these as well as the sort of multiple intelligences that Gardner covers: rhythmic, spatial, linguistic, mathematical, kinesthetic, intra- and inter-personal, naturalistic, and existential.

What thrivable world becomes possible with these expanded and acknowledged capabilities when we honor and embrace them? When we recognize that different people have different capabilities and we honor and embrace them all? When we recognize the prejudice that values a specific IQ over the others – like it valued men over women and white skin over other colors. What world can we create when we acknowledge the full spectrum of our intelligence and awareness collectively? Does the recognition of multiple forms of intelligence call forth greater curiosity and creativity from us all? Shifting to a thrivable world is going to take more than the intelligence acknowledged and appreciated in the age of rationality. It will take the celebration of the whole mind and the whole range of capabilities that humans have to face the challenges ahead.

Plasticity

Adjusting to this evolving world requires new and old to continue learning and evolving. The traditional view of the brain assumed that the neural connections formed rapidly in childhood became fixed in adulthood and deteriorated in old age. But recent neuroscience research reveals that human brains are plastic, adjusting through time, and forming new connections. Our brains evolve as we use them, adjusting through our experiences. They can even develop and adapt significantly. Deterioration comes from lack of use and stimulation, rather than being purely a consequence of age. Using your brain can grow your potential in a virtuous cycle opening up more and more possibility. Learning how to make our brains more plastic fosters transformation through increased flexibility, growth, and integration.

When we view our brains as adaptable and able to expand possibility, we can put more faith in ourselves to adapt to challenges and expand our ability to make connections with others (and track all the information that requires). Not only can this help us to live more thriving lives, it can help us to adapt to the world as we co-create it together, increasing our collective resilience.

Takeaway

We are meaning-making beings. And we are not only greedy and sometimes rational actors; we are also compassionate and irrational. Understanding ourselves as empathic and connected beings in search of meaning and purpose, energized by mastery and autonomy, enables us to create the world around us in new ways. We can refresh our models of how humans operate. Instead of designing games so we don't lose, we can begin to design for more winning all around. We can navigate better. We can navigate to where we fit and help others fit around us. We can shift away from focusing solely on our limitations and avoiding worst possible scenarios and move toward a broader view of humans as actors with positive intent. Reward yourself by helping others and exposing yourself to places where others are being helped. Let other people help you. A smart hedonist is a helpful one.

We are humans who can be encouraged by being given opportunities to make a contribution to the world and those around us.

We have relatively small, slow, conscious minds and immense, fast, unconscious minds. How will you design your life around this understanding? When will you use slow thinking? How will you encourage more play in your life?

While there will still be times when we act from greed or scarcity, there is a growing possibility of acting from trust. We can indeed be altruistic. Where will you play with others from a space of trusting yourself and other people to have positive intent?

Without mistaking autonomy for individualism, we can work toward a greater purpose for ourselves and society at large.

Happiness in the hedonistic sense is highly relative. More than that, be mindful that humans are terrible judges of what will bring them future happiness. Maybe we should be a lot more rational – and slow thinking – about happiness. When we focus on the benefits of a possible future instead of on what is required of us to stop doing something 'bad' that we already do, then we lubricate the process of creating a world we want. We know more about what makes people feel fulfilled even if they themselves can't feel into it at the time. How can you gift those around you with the joy of purpose?

Be inspirational and share how you have transformed the pain of your experience into purposeful action.

As we increase our understanding of what gives us a sense of purpose and what matters to us as individuals and as communities and societies, that self-awareness enables us to make better informed choices about how we do what we do, when we can do it together, and what that can bring us emotionally and psychologically. We can face our fears with more strength, knowing that even trauma can bring out our strengths and we can adapt to what happens to us.

We learn to tap into a greater sense and breadth of our intelligence as well as into the benefits of the diversity in that intelligence that exists across the population at large. And, thanks to neuroplasticity, we can adjust our brains as we go through life, expanding our possibilities individually and collectively.

Make a thrivable world for yourself and those around you by bringing forward the intention to playfully create a powerful purpose: thriving. And...

Level up! \o/

CHAPTER 6

Social Revolutions

We are, of course, social creatures. And neuroscience and behavioral economics confirm that. However, not only are we social, but our social behavior is evolving. The Social Revolution unfolding is not simply social media. Nilofer Merchant calls this the Social Era. It includes shifts in our understanding of leadership, how we perceive diversity, what processes we use together, the infrastructure we rely on, our education methods, governance options, markets, and even health. Some of what follows points to innovations, while some points to discoveries – but together it forms a series of important breakthroughs. For example, Nicholas Christakis and James Fowler recently surprised many people by showing how being overweight or happy can be socially contagious.

Also, at this layer of the social, consider the weaving of social connection by shared experience through time. Simply put, a generation shares an experience. I believe that there is an important convergence between the different generations on their paths together. If you visit someone born before WWII, you will likely find that they save, re-use, and recycle things: paper, aluminum foil, bottles. All these 'green' practices are things they have done for much of their lives. Continuing to paint generations with broad brush strokes, the Boomers are shifting into retirement. At this point, they are turning their attention toward building lives of purpose after a few decades of building personal wealth. But the generation stereotype is of the hippie who joined mass civil rights movements that made huge strides in social justice. I believe that drive for justice is still in the Boomers, and it will show up more as they move into volunteering and purpose-filled retirement.

I am Generation X and our generation offers a narrow bridge between the Boomers and Millennials. Broadly speaking, Gen X resists authority and represents the age of punk culture. We grew up in the shadow of crisis: not just the cold war, but also the death (actual or metaphorical) of heroes and leaders: Kennedy and King, O.J. Simpson and Kurt Cobain. It makes us skeptical of trusting figureheads for very long, even good ones. On the upside, we also were influenced by the fall of the Berlin Wall. Our post-modern sense of irony and anarchy still permeates much of what we do. Many of us tried to have it all, purpose and power, but we've had internal conflicts over the whole thing.

The Millennials are growing up in a story that says they don't have to choose between doing good and making a living. They struggle less with marking individual identity the way Gen X did. Instead, they seem more comfortable acting in hives, swarms, collectives. And they may need those skills to make it through the work world today, as they struggle to find jobs. Millennials are digital natives – in fact they are internet natives, expecting the world to be more like the internet – interconnected, social, sharing. Making the world better, for Millennials, seems to be less an act of resistance (which it is for us punk Gen Xers) and more an act of creation and integrity. From my perspective, they embody the Buckminster Fuller maxim, "You never change things by fighting the existing reality. To change something, build a new model that makes the existing model obsolete."

I believe each of these generations strives, with its individual strengths and maturity, to reach for thriving, even as each has a different story about how the world works. That is not to say there aren't conflicts. Boomers tend, in general, not to recognize the way leadership works among the Millennials, for example. And Millennials are not getting adequate mentoring from Boomers who think the myths of the 1950s-70s might still be true (get a degree and you are assured a career... the economy grows, so business should grow, standard of living is increasing, etc.) Millennials have grand and enthusiastic ideas of youth without the wisdom of experiencing the complicated factors that their elders have learned to work with and around. Even with all the conflicts and misunderstandings, I deeply believe that there is enough coherence across the generations to shift the human story to one of thriving.

Collective cultural evolution is, of course, always in process, regardless of the generation you belong to. At times, as at sea where wind, tide, and current can synch to produce rogue waves, the energy of different generations can combine to produce extraordinary efforts and results – way outside the usual norms. Once again, I don't claim this is happening, but it could happen in response to the perfect storm of crises that we face – meaning that the usual projections could be radically off when they suggest what the future will look like by extending forward our current trajectories.

If collective will has been distributed broadly across many spaces with many interests and maturity levels, what might be possible if there was a moment when that attention synced up?

Communication Revolution

The social media and communication revolution documented by *Here Comes Everybody, Cognitive Surplus, Wikinomics,* and a bookcase more, reveal how the revolution in communication media is leading to everyone being able to be a producer, as well as a consumer, of content. As well as commonly expressed concerns about porn or lolcats, we can also think positively about these new media acting as a play space. In this space we can stumble through new ways of interacting with one another, and we can display our individual natures and our collective capacities.

We struggle to learn new social graces as we interact in barely defined spaces – containers that often don't have clear rules or principles of behavior.

Speaking with Jo Guldi, a historian at the Harvard Society of Fellows, I was interested to hear her liken this to the shift in culture at the beginning of the 20th century as more people moved to cities. Then, Emily Post's etiquette book was the much needed behavioral guide for an emerging culture. In the same way, we develop the norms and practices for these new ways of being and creating together in digital environments. There are tons of digital 'etiquette' books out there, helping us learn what to expect and what is acceptable to do in online social contexts.

These new ways of coming together generate cascading ripples of impact across just about every area of human engagement. Knowledge flows, while not yet efficient, move more quickly and more often to appropriate people. Many people feel more empowered to produce content (for better or worse at the individual level), but in a longer term view, we develop innovative ways to distinguish the noise from the signal.

Hashtags are an example of this. In the early days of Twitter, Chris Messina used the # sign to indicate a topic, and the use of it spread. Now I can find nuggets based on searching a hashtag that a group agrees to or builds on. I don't have to follow everything that everyone is saying. I only need to track the tag. Thousands of innovators are putting attention on finding the signal in the noise of the very noisy internet as ever more people become producers there.

However, the digital divide sharpens. For digital natives, if it isn't online; it doesn't exist. I say this because I have caught myself thinking this way. If I can't find a local store online, then to me it is as if it doesn't exist. I can't find it. I won't be walking around a mall or down the street and discover it. I get all my news online, fed by a rich stream of social connections that filter the world for me, so I won't see it in the local paper. I don't call a restaurant to find out if they are open. I check the web. More than that, I search my social network by asking their opinion. On the other hand, my Dad doesn't even use a computer. I have to actively work to remember what navigating the world without the internet looked like. He has to know the location of a place and directions on how to get there before he gets in the car because he doesn't have a phone with a map of the entire world on it. He goes to a book store and looks on the shelf for the book he saw in the paper magazine he was reading. For those, like my Dad, who had to learn (or haven't learned) the technology, very little exists online. My Dad just can't imagine, when he stops by my office, that I am speaking at my computer to talk with someone in South Africa. I have acclimated in the last 15 years to this online world. He hasn't. It isn't just my Dad, it is people without access to computers, the internet, and smart phones. This population might be dwindling, but it important not to leave them behind as we strive together for a world of greater thriving. We must be careful not to assume that the social web has touched everyone and we must be mindful of who we might be leaving behind.

Consider how much computers, cell phones, and the internet have radically reshaped our world in a decade or two. If you think we can't change and adapt quickly, virally, at a global scale, here is your counter example. We have. And we can again. We are. That doesn't mean it isn't messy, and we need to keep in mind who is included and not included in the shift. Transformation usually involves loss. The butterfly lost the ability to be a caterpillar, but in so doing, gained the ability to fly.

Social Business

This social revolution has rolling impacts for business too. Businesses that once could only push their message out to a world of passive consumers now contend with public messages about themselves. We witness the thoughts of our peers about the businesses they like and don't like. We share our stories about companies – and as companies move into the social space, they interact and begin to pull those messages in as feedback and insight into their work.

Those that resist this shift risk being seen as irrelevant or outdated. If they refuse to engage in the 'social conversation' online, they aren't even perceived for social selection. And if they cling to the one-way monologue of 20th century marketing, many customers will feel like they are getting yelled at as they walk through the virtual market. The world becomes more and more based in relationships. And relationships are grounded in conversation. To survive in this new social context, companies move into conversational marketing.

So companies must contend with new social organisms with collective will and power at a time when their own social organisms are shrinking from down-sizing. They listen to their buyers as part of their research and development, as well as inviting buyers and potential buyers to be advocates for their brands and offerings.

Innovative companies learn how to connect to these collectives of buyers so as to blur the boundaries between those inside and outside the company.

Think of how Apple fans become attached to their devices so rapidly that there is a peer pressure (at least in the geek world) to buy Apple products. Apple doesn't have to pay its fans. It just has to please them (which might be harder – fans of brands and products can be quite fickle).

One problem for companies is the threat, not from traditional competitors but from networks. Leaderless organisms that co-create goods and services outside the boundaries of the paying market. Open sourcing can be highly productive with a resource efficiency that hierarchical bricks and mortar companies can't compete with. And, where open source sometimes fails to manage design and user interface well, other open models exist that conflict with the very form that conventional companies take. Think of Napster. We move from the model of the factory – with clear hierarchies and decision-making structures – toward fluid and organic networks of production and sharing. The benefits achieved in the move from factory production to network production parallel the gains in efficiency and effectiveness achieved when first we moved from craft production to factory production more than two centuries ago. Where factory production increased productivity and output, network production increases variety – the ability to customize and offer bespoke solutions. All three models have optimal production at different scales.

The emergence of network production takes us toward a transformation in leadership and organizational structure as more efficient (network) production methods drive out the competition.

Leading and Leaderless Organisms

Leadership, as I grew up thinking of it – in oversimplified terms – had someone in control at the top dictating to everyone below what to do and how to do it. A good leader could inspire productive cooperation among his 'followers' to actualize what he dictated. Command and control made sense in a world where we thought of people as machines. We needed leadership like that to move us to work together to produce, especially in factory-like settings. Factory production gave rise to factory-like leadership. And factory-like leadership increased efficiencies in the system. Typically it produced an upward spiral of optimization that eventually toppled over into bureaucracy with a downward spiral of decreasing effectiveness. We are just now realizing scaling concerns as research reveals that companies decrease efficiency when they exceed a certain count of employees. The effort to manage and connect those employees burdens the company in ways that exceed the 'economies of scale' benefits of production through size. While this might be true for hierarchical organizations, it won't be true for networks, because they don't have the management overhead.

Knowledge work requires a different style of leadership. The same is true if you want people to genuinely contribute their best performances and feel loyal to what they are doing. As Jim Collins says, "get the right people on the bus in the right seats." He also talks significantly about level 5 leadership. Jim argues that it takes a level 5 leader to make a good company great. What makes a level 5 leader? Humility and passionate professional will and not big charisma. Because a level 5 leader isn't after attention for herself. She humbly shares her story of what the collective can do together and gets everyone aligned with that story. Look at Mozilla, for example, which has thousands of volunteers working to build a more open web, including the browser Firefox. Mitchell Baker and her collaborators achieved that worldwide community effort by telling a story of possibility that people committed to, so compelling that even (and especially) people who were not paid pitched in. They are now 15 years in and part of a growing global organization.

In the age of our current Social Revolution, progressive organizations have leadership structures that come in two basic forms: one relies on Champions and the other is the Leaderless Organization. Early seeds of this thinking were to be found in the work of people like Robert Greenleaf *(Servant Leadership)* and, later, Peter Block – before the internet had much scale at all. However, the participatory and empowering nature of the internet has resulted in more champion/advocate leaders.

Try it:

Reflect on your experience with leaders.

- ⊤ What do you notice about the ones you were most willing to give your very best to?

- ⊤ Which ones did you resist? What do you notice about your resistance to them?

- ⊤ In what contexts have you felt the most free to take actions of your choosing? What did leadership look like there?

- ⊤ When a leader you worked with made the work about your success or about group success rather than their own agenda or pride, did that impact your contribution?

- ⊤ Where has someone expressed gratitude for your efforts? How did that impact your behavior?

Champions

In the knowledge and experience economy, a champion who can bring out the best in the individual and team through encouragement, acknowledgement and shared goals inspires better quality contributions and greater loyalty. This is crucial because, in knowledge and creativity work, we are asking people to use their minds. It is difficult to perceive action or inaction. Can you tell when someone is trying to use their mind? How do you enforce the using of minds? Leaders can't command minds the way they can command bodies. Rather, they can only invite, nurture, and reward the use of minds in creative work. Thus, relationships matter immensely.

The degree to which people give over their minds to work on projects strongly correlates to their relationship with the people they work with and are coordinated by.

This makes necessary the shift from a leadership model based on command and control to one based on nurturing, encouragement, and relationship.

Furthermore, in systems of networked production, command and control methods of leadership fail completely. In their place, it is clear and aligned shared purpose that drives the production process. A champion acts as the flag bearer for the purpose. A nurturing champion also continuously pushes acknowledgement of effort out to the edges, giving credit for progress to others through the organization. And a nurturing champion acknowledges and encourages the best in everyone around her, operating from a belief that everyone has something to contribute to the shared purpose. Thus, people working with nurturing champions experience more autonomy through an experience of being trusted to do what they do best.

Leaderless Organizations

The seemingly leaderless organization – or organism – is a form of leadership that many people don't perceive at all. Ori Brafman and Rod A. Beckstrom point to these strange organisms in *The Starfish and the Spider: The Unstoppable Power of Leaderless Organizations*.

In a starfish organization, while a person may seem to be the temporary head of the activity, removing them has little impact on the organism as a whole. For example, the evolution of shared music started with Napster. The more organizations that made music shareable were shut down, the more resilient the next iteration became until it was so diffuse it couldn't be shut down. (The dark side of this anti-fragility shows up in terrorist networks.)

It's not that people have stopped leading activities. Instead, it seems like the leading is temporary. The instigator acts as a catalyst by exciting people about an idea and then releasing the work and participants to continue to evolve on their own. If command and control leadership can be likened to the care and grooming of a bonsai tree, the leaderless organization is more like guerilla gardening (mix up some seeds and dirt and toss them somewhere they just might flourish). It isn't about managing a process. It is about the seed that creates coherence for collective action: an idea.

The starfish organization is a particular form of 'leaderless' organization: it appears to be led by an idea rather than a leader.

Current movements for creating social change and building a better world often have these qualities of the leaderless organization too. While any organization or individual leader in the sector can be removed or sidelined, the movement as a whole continues to grow and become more agile and resilient. Leaderless organizations can seem less visible because they lack a figurehead to speak on their behalf, but they are much more resilient because that figurehead can't be eradicated to stifle the movement. Anyone involved has the power to step forward and lead.

Consider the two levels of a system. We can ask what is happening to a car (moving forward, stopped, moving back or turning, etc.) and we can ask what is happening to traffic as a whole. The domain a leader can effectively control is in the realm of the car. The way to influence the flow of traffic is with a leaderless organization 'driven' by a shared goal – it is like being swarmed by a motorcycle cavalcade or a convoy of trucks.

These new leadership strategies – Champions and Leaderless Organizations – help us to evolve our ability to activate and produce, bringing out the things we need most: better cooperation, better results, greater productivity, enduring connection and commitment to each other, enduring visions, more organic organisms/organizations, and at the heart, more satisfied people. And that is crucial for a thrivable world.

The shift in leadership to champion level 5 leadership brings thriving into organizations and makes it more possible for the organization to be agile and adaptable in the marketplace. More than that, when we are appreciated for our contributions at work we are more satisfied and more inspired to contribute. Businesses that manage to encourage us to excel, to allow us to direct ourselves in our work and inspire us with a sense of purpose come closer to achieving the triumvirate of human motivation: autonomy, mastery, and purpose. This triumvirate tends to be very alive and flourishing when we see a leaderless network organism in action. The energy generated from the triumvirate is significant enough to overcome the lack of financial compensation for many of the people involved. Which is an important part of what makes it hard for traditional business to compete with them. Join together autonomy, mastery and purpose and…

Level up!

Companies Enter the Social Era

Social business isn't just marketing, it can involve any and all areas of a business. Companies may not look like they did before. Shifts in organizational structures reflect the new ways that people are communicating and socializing.

I met with Nilofer Merchant, who writes about the Social Era. She has that high level executive energy about her, as if her brain is processing five different layers of information at once and precisely executing on her optimal choices. At the same time, she expresses open curiosity, engages as a peer in challenging conversations, and really strives to live her story. Upon meeting her, I became an ardent fan. She writes, "Lean, adaptive community-driven organizations built for speed, will thrive." This is tied to her gorilla and gazelles metaphor (comparing an 800lb. goliath with an agile herd of 800 gazelles).

There is a deep need for agility in a shifting world. Strangely, the illusion of solid boundaries between what is inside and what is outside the firm dissolves. Semi-permeable membranes operate within network relationships. Tasks once done by insiders or even consulting firms might become conversations directly with clients and consumers.

Merchant goes on, "When you have shared purpose, it doesn't matter how many people work 'in the company' and how many work 'with' the company or how many are serving as an army of volunteers who want to advance the mission.... Organizations will not need to be big to have a big impact. But they will need an extremely clear purpose, and shared, decentralized power throughout. When a clear purpose is coupled with shared power, people can self-organize to reach the goal."

Old management models were designed to work in factory production settings. They often do not apply in the Social Era where, as Merchant says, "Organizations can be in a constant conversation to learn what is working and what is not, and adapt on the fly. These nimble organizations consistently try new things, adapt to what works and thus improve the bottom line."

In her final Harvard Business Blog post on the Social Era, Nilofer Merchant offers a chart of shifts in business practices for this era with examples of each. Here it is:

Area	Traditional	Social Era Business Models	Example
HR	Employees	Curators/Co-Creators	Singularity University
Service	Call Centers	Peer Communities	McAfee
Capitalization	A Few Big Investors	Crowdfunding	KickStarter
Product	Mass Production	Custom Production	Desktop Factory
Distribution	Partnership Contracts	Open Marketplaces	Etsy
Supply Chain	Middlemen and Warehouses	User-Driven Production	Lego Factory
Sales	Sales Team Incentives	Customer Love	Evernote
Marketing	Big Budget	Passionate Users	TED/TEDx

As we adapt in the Social Era, more efficient and productive organizations and collections of producers are self-organizing. But this also generates tighter feedback loops in human systems, creating more responsiveness and 'humanness' in the business sector. The Social Era creates a shift in capitalism itself, making it more relationship-centric, more humane, and adjusting the balance of power in the triumvirate of business, government, and citizens.

The entire system rebalances itself.

It is not the end of capitalism, it is the end of a form of capitalism that wasn't responsible to the larger whole, wasn't responsible to the ecosystems it acted parasitically on. Social media and the emerging ways of the social era make more visible the 'invisible hand' and carry public commentary on (and ridicule for) the 'invisible foot' that companies were using to control the culture. This new form of more humane capitalism means that businesses that improve the talent and quality of the people who work for and with them will succeed better over the long run. And more successful businesses are now minding their externalities (because even with long feedback loops, they know the externalities come back to them in the form of social support or criticism).

Network Organisms

At the same time, organizations and networks are forming with new structures – I have already mentioned open source software groups, for example. Clearly, communication modes change and there is a domino effect on relationships of every sort among businesses, governments, nonprofits, and community groups. Networks are formed.

Let's call these groups that are able to be productive together, network organisms.

Some of this shift comes from the gritty reality of corporate down-sizing. Some of the shift comes from the opportunities that technology enables. And some comes from a change in cultural expectations. Whatever the cause, the old business and organizational models are in flux: many are somewhere between the old model and the new. Often there are internal tensions in those organizations between individuals old enough to have known a different world, and a younger, technology-enabled generation with new ideas about how organizations operate. This is where the friction is.

Collaboration seems like a trending word, but the grace to work together well in new organizational forms has yet to arrive. It will, in time. Collaboration isn't the answer to all our problems. And collaborating, while often being celebrated, can be challenging to do well.

Nor is one business framework right for every operation. As the paradigm shifts, clarity will emerge about where, when, and how to collaborate (and when not to). We will learn which forms of working with others fit which situations.

The film industry makes an excellent and familiar example of these temporary, highly productive network organisms. Sometimes a film team generates a company just for that single film. Various people and organizations come together, make a film, and then disaggregate. There is no expectation that the company lasts forever or gets ever bigger. The process is highly organic in a high stakes market.

Companies are simply structures we put in place to get work done together more efficiently. But companies with rigid structures can't adapt at the pace of an agile learning, amoeba-like network. A thriving world emerges from this transformation of rigid organizational structures to organic networks because people seek purpose, autonomy, and mastery. Individual producers can achieve all three more easily when they are not being commanded and controlled.

Thriving Network Organisms

Let's mix some physics and biology metaphors. If you imagine the core of a network as the attractor force for the body of the network, there needs to be enough pull to draw people in. And, the network needs people on the periphery spreading out in search of new information and connections. The core is focused on similarity. How are we alike? What holds us together? And the periphery is focused on what we can discover.

In the thrivable world that is emerging, key strengths for networks are: agility/adaptability, resilience, openness, and diversity.

A thriving network acts like a slime mold, which we have seen can exist both as a single organism and band together to form a collective organism. As the slime mold encounters changes in the environment, it shifts form. Thriving networks also demonstrate this agile ability to shape shift depending on their context. Crucial to the health of the network organism is diversity.

Diversity

A network organism coheres by virtue of an acknowledgment of a similarity. What is it that the network shares as the same? A geo-location? A passion for growing tomatoes? A commitment to a method, practice, or belief? Fanaticism for a platform, like Apple or Android? This coherence lives most visibly at the core of the network. However, the ability for that network to be agile and evolve depends on it also taking advantage of differences. So when I use the term diversity, I mean it in a very Darwinian sense of the benefits of bio-diversity and much less in a civil rights sense.

The last thirty years have also seen an important shift in the social need for diversity. It is not about head count and skin color. It is about resilience and adaptability.

Diversity may have begun as a moral or ethical issue, but it's become a practical and strategic one.

I have been inspired repeatedly by Deanna Zandt, author of *Share This*. When I think of her, a photograph comes to mind where she is giggling with Baratunde Thurston (of *The Onion*). Her pale whiteness with platinum hair wildly punk next to his laughter-infused, dark-skinned face. Deanna has worked for decades on social justice issues. She brings a rich sense of humor to everything she does. I asked her to write in the *Thrivability Sketch*, because she had such a clear sense that the value diversity brings is so much more juicy than the moralistic arguments people make to enforce it. Deanna Zandt writes:

"Creating a just and thrivable society is sort of like the evolution of a species. If you have a bunch of the same DNA mixing together, the species mutates poorly and eventually dies off. But bring in variety – new strains of DNA – and you create a stronger species."

It's no different in idea generation. Get a bunch of like-minded people talking to each other and you will get the same results as you would if you only had two of them. But get a wide variety of differently-minded people all committed to the same goal, and you can get more and better ideas. This is in many ways why Wikipedia is better than your typical encyclopedia. It is not just that it gets volunteers to contribute – it gets volunteers from a broad range of expertise, interests, and capabilities. You might be surprised by what can happen. Who would have guessed that having women on boards made a difference to the bottom line? Sure some might have argued for it morally, but would you have guessed that it brought something to the business that mattered?

Nilofer Merchant wrote about women and boards as she became a director:

"Consider the findings of Catalyst's study of Fortune 500 companies:

Return on Equity: On average, companies with the highest percentages of women board directors outperformed those with the least by 53 percent.

Return on Sales: On average, companies with the highest percentages of women board directors outperformed those with the least by 42 percent.

Return on Invested Capital: On average, companies with the highest percentages of women board directors outperformed those with the least by 66 percent.

There is also evidence that women are more effective as board members. Reuters described this as the 'diamond skirt' phenomenon: among other things, women do more homework before board meetings and cause higher attendance rates overall.

Many have argued it just makes good business sense to create diversity."

This is not merely about women, it is about many forms of diversity. These benefits might be caused by the women present or they may be simply a result of the openness that led to women being included. Whatever the cause, the correlation is valuable.

We are becoming much wiser about listening to other voices to expand our awareness, perceive the world from other vantage points, and tap into creativity from other ways of thinking.

Openness matters. This might be from diversity of sex, age, spiritual tradition, culture, or class. When we step away from the moral argument about diversity and look at the practical benefits of it, even in our self-interest we must recognize the value it can bring us. A new social order emerges from this pragmatic approach that has greater resilience, creativity, and productive output. It becomes more thrivable.

Building the Social Era

As I was exploring all the facets of the Social Era, I had to wonder, what is making all of this possible now? I think there is a convergence of breakthroughs that come together to make this new Social Era possible. First, there have been innovations in the processes we use together. Second, the web is enabling trust to be more visible and scale to much larger numbers, Third, the underlying infrastructure has 'social' principles at its very core.

Group Process

As Valdis Krebs says regularly: "Connect on your similarities and profit from your differences." So, how do we work together with people who are different from us? How do we connect? What process do we use? We are still finding new ways to do group work in the Social Era.

The last thirty years has seen a magnificent transformation in group process arts: the methods we use to work together to produce collective goods and ideas. These range from Open Space and World Café to Citizen Deliberative Councils and Asset Based Community Development. To get a sense of just how much has been generated for group process, open up *The Change Handbook: The Definitive Resource on Today's Best Methods for Engaging Whole Systems*. Never before have we had such a breadth of process tools with which to engage others and move through together for collective outcomes. We learn together the various knobs and dials we can adjust to better achieve our outcomes given the values and beliefs we hold and the group we have convened in the time we have allotted to be together.

This coming together to form network organisms challenges us. We are confronted by the differences between individuals even as we come together in common purpose. Having processes that help us to navigate those differences and provide social containers for producing work together acts as a lubricant to the social organism – reducing friction between people and allowing more work to be generated together.

Trust

Working together requires trust. When we change the story we are telling about ourselves, so that humans are no longer seen as purely rational, greedy, self-interested actors but primarily as caring, empathic, generous, altruistic ones, we begin to shift our ability to trust each other. Or what it means to trust begins to change. I may have trusted you to behave in a greedy way, and thus avoided interacting with you or made sure we had binding legal contracts before engaging. If instead, I trust that you have positive intentions and may want to participate in something larger than your own self-interest, I become more willing to try things with you.

Try it:

⊤   List five people that you trust. Then describe what you trust them for. Are there differences? What would you not trust each of these people for?

⊤   List five people you don't trust. Are there differences? What would you trust these people for?

From a different angle, trust improbably emerges online. It may appear counter-intuitive to trust people online whom you have never met, can't see, and who may not even be using their real names. However, online tools have developed ways to show whether enough trust can be present for a particular interaction or transaction.

We still oversimplify trust and treat it as something that can be turned on or off.

Trust isn't binary. In practice, I may trust you with my car but not my secrets, my apartment but not my children. And the way we build trust is by taking the risk of trusting someone. As they prove trustworthy, we may risk more with them.

Nor is trust necessarily transitive: if I trust you and you trust Arthur, it may not follow that I trust Arthur. However, I may be more willing to trust Arthur when you tell me that you trust him, and especially if you tell me why you trust him, what you have trusted him for in the past, and what happened when you did. We are all familiar with this in the practices we have around referrals and testimonials.

The way online interactions have transformed this space is not by increasing our ability to trust or by changing how trust operates, but by showing us how trustworthy someone is by using tracking mechanisms for behavior in a specific context.

We trust the tracking mechanisms, we rely on the data they provide to test out, in small experiments, our trust in others.

A critical component of this is what we have learned about the wisdom and madness of crowds. If I can't see other people's answers and I guess, say, 'how many jelly beans are in the jar,' my answer, averaged with enough other guesses, will be very close to the right answer. However, if I can see other people's guesses, I am usually unduly influenced by those answers, and the wisdom of the crowd fails. Still, if I see on Yelp that 150 people rated a restaurant highly, I am more likely to believe it is a good restaurant. There are a wide variety of ways we play this out, and some of them work very effectively.

Others, over time, reveal biases that undermine collective wisdom. For example, eBay's rating system is not double blind. So if I see how you rate me, it will impact how I rate you back. Most people, wanting a good rating, will give someone a better rating than they might deserve to ensure that they get a good rating in return.

Still, while systems like eBay's have points of occasional failure, they are believable enough and there are few enough failures that billions of dollars are transacted over these trust-mediating systems. Web-based systems like Couchsurfing closely monitor reporting of negative experiences, and like any smart customer-driven organization, act very proactively to address and remedy those negative experiences – thus they become more trustable and the exchanges visible online become trustworthy too.

Note that trust is so crucial to our economic engagement that when trust in the monetary system falters, we have recessions and even depressions. And while we can all theorize about where we went wrong in breaking the trust in the flows of our economy and money, the recovery depends deeply on regaining or rebuilding trust – however that happens. Scott Reynolds Nelson is an economic and labor historian. He lived above me while he was in Chicago on a Newbury Library Fellowship. I had never met anyone so clearly thriving on days immersed in the library digging up information from a century ago. He was writing *A Nation of Deadbeats: An Uncommon History of America's Financial Disasters* at the time. He would come over with delicious craft beer and share with me his discoveries that week. I asked him to share one such story for the *Thrivability Sketch*. He writes about trust and blockage:

> "When the Panic of 1857 hit with the failure of a bank called Ohio Life Insurance and Trust Company, Elizur [Wright] was prepared. This blockage of trade and transport, Wright declared, was a result of distrust. Insurance companies needed reliable accounting practices that would allow Massachusetts to calculate net present value, and internal rate of return. When trust returns, Wright assured them, the blockage will be over....The panic was short-lived, and Elizur Wright's accounting principles became the basis of what we now call Generally Accepted Accounting Principles, adopted by millions of companies, states, and non-governmental organizations throughout the world."

Nelson concludes that, "Wright took advantage of blockage to identify its root cause – a distrust of opacity. Increased financial transparency was the solution; trust collapses without it. Blockage can let us make institutions open up and make them thrivable."

Social Infrastructures

When your neighbor is a landscape historian, and you share a few conversations, it can change what you see in the world. In my case, I then also started having conversations with Bice Wilson of Meridian Design, a New York architecture firm, about placemaking. So I started to notice, when traveling through different spaces in the physical world, which ones are conducive to conversation. For example, suburbs with lots of fences, few sidewalks, and low walkability discourage us from engaging with those around us. We don't have the immediacy of seeing people in the personal realms of their backyards (and sometimes even the fronts). We don't stop to talk with them on the street because everyone is driving everywhere. And the social spaces of downtown shops, local parks, and center squares are ghost towns in the rust-belt of the Midwest.

There is a growing awareness of design for place-making and social activities, both in work contexts and in home and civil contexts. New home developments focus on walkability, neighborliness, and areas for social convening. Re-developing public social spaces and downtowns has been a growing trend in recent years. And the most notable changes come from social environments at work. There is a move away from the isolated cubicle and office, and toward flexible work spaces and more collaborative work options. Indeed, the whole co-working movement taps into this social need.

As we learn more about how effective collaborations happen, we begin designing social infrastructure to support it.

This is also true for the online environment. The social forums of the 90s developed the key conditions needed for community engagement, participation, and cooperation. With Web 2.0, we have seen these technologies scale up. Online infrastructures lack some of the implicit relationship-building, intimacy-creating, and trust-making features that we find face-to-face, yet they evolve each year to come closer to transcending these challenges.

Rising from the ashes of the factory-like infrastructure we built around us, we see both physical and digital construction of spaces for social engagement. We are more than machines and robots. We talk. We share. And if we don't have spaces to do that, we will make them.

Outside business, the Social Era is generating a more thriving world.

Social media certainly got enough press to be considered a revolution by itself. But the social era shift is bigger than social media, as Nilofer Merchant shows us. Being more social comes from having new processes, new ways of mediating trust, and infrastructure that supports conversation and connectivity. It isn't just changing people's lives where they are working in, or served by, businesses and organizations. It is transforming government and education, and creating new markets.

Governance in an Era of Connectivity

My mother, who is not a digital native, was looking at something on my laptop and tried to swipe the screen as if it was an iPad (which she doesn't even have!). But she is so familiar now with touch screen devices that, for a moment, she forgot this wasn't one. Similarly, those of us living online become accustomed to the culture there. We begin expecting more of our world to operate with the same social dynamics and governance mechanisms.

If you get used to being on a wiki where you can edit anything you see needs editing, you start to wonder why the rest of the world isn't editable. If you are used to making your own videos and writing your own content to share with the world, you wonder why you can't be a citizen in the same engaged and active way.

When you get used to using a search tool to find a good restaurant, read reviews of a movie, buy your flight to NYC or your tickets to the concert, or read a favorite magazine, you start to wonder why you can't search government data to find out about local financial activity, crime statistics, and policy decisions or pay your parking tickets, renew your license, register to vote, and reserve your camping spot with the DNR.

In the social world of Web 2.0 you don't just do these things – you also talk about them with other people. You go online and talk to people about a restaurant. You look at other people's conversations about a movie you want to see. You look at what other people paid for the flights you want. You arrange car-share with people going to the concert. You comment on your favorite blog. You become used to that. So, again, you wonder why we aren't talking about and sharing our experiences of government financial activity, local crime stats, housing, environment, jobs, taxes, and transportation. Well it's happening. There are apps for this. And the apps are linking up.

Governments are opening up information. Some eagerly. Some hesitantly. Right now, the openness is focused on data coming out via the transparency movement, and on the ability to be social with the data. This is Gov 2.0.

Behind all this is a movement of people interested in participatory democracy. It could change how we vote, not just who we vote for. Often well versed in process arts and deeply experienced in government methods, those leading the charge for participatory democracy could lead to the most radical changes in how governments operate around the world. If you are one of the many who believe that the government has become a behemoth with the wrong incentives that makes the world less thrivable rather than more, get ready for a phase change.

In this social revolution, the taste of participation and the addictive effects of socializing combine to pollinate every aspect of our lives. No nation will be left untouched by it.

Changing business via social media was a small step. Changing government that way is a big step. And it is already in process. That the change will come is inevitable. The form it will take is not yet clear. The tap tapping of millions of fingers writing billions of words and linking terabytes of citizen data has a supernova feel, doesn't it? Once we get good at it. We don't have it right yet. News of the NSA spying on citizens may seem like a setback, but I see it as kindling the passion of US citizens for a new way of running government. We may lose some powerful voices who make sacrifices for the whole to be changed, like Assange or Snowden, but the movement they are a part of is a starfish that will carry on, swarm over, and mutate the way governments are run. You can see already the fear of governments across the world as we watch dictators try to shut down, shut out, or control the anti-fragile system that makes up the social connection of the internet.

Education in a Social World

The social revolution is also beginning to infiltrate the education system. The game dynamics of incentives and punishments in the education system in the United States has set up schools to fail. Worse that that, it has set up young boys in particular to fail. The schools need kids to pass tests and show proficiencies. To do that, teachers need kids to face forward, listen, and learn quickly through mostly verbal information. That's something girls tend to do better at than boys, who tend to be more kinesthetic – they need to learn through action. Kids who can't sit still, listen intently, or follow directions for 7 hours get the label of 'ADHD' so they can be medicated to behave appropriately.

My kids are in this system. My daughter is a star student – straight As. Last term she even brought home an A+ because she hadn't missed a single point on a test. My son, equally bright but with a different learning style, struggles to get Cs. It is incredibly frustrating to see a smart child develop a story about being dumb because he can't make the grades. I am not alone. Parents across the country are frustrated by this.

One dad decided to make a video to teach his son math. Thus was born the Khan Academy. Today it lists over 86,000,000 lessons delivered. Learning is delivered in 10-minute chunks, completion of work results in awards, stats are delivered to the user, knowledge is mapped to grasp the context of learning and pathways through material are self-selected. No, it isn't quite social yet – as in learners working with other learners – but the future of learning will be social.

There are other efforts to remake education systems. I went for a walk through Crissy Field in San Francisco with Dale Dougherty. Dale is the co-founder of O'Reilly Media and the man behind *Make Magazine* and Maker Faire events. He is a very hands-on guy, and you can feel his passion as he talks about the power of making. This is a guy who literally makes his own dogfood. He asked me, "What if the evidence of learning wasn't a test. What if it was something that was made?" The craft culture in the world of *Make* means that originality is valued, customization applauded, and functional use is celebrated. Sharing what works and what doesn't feeds the social aspect of making.

We learn to make together. We make prototypes, share, and iterate.

The future of learning in a thrivable world will be driven by self-pacing activities matched to the user's learning style and appropriate for brains rewired by games and a world of rapid and constant change. It will be less important that facts are known (as facts are easily searched) and more important to be adept at the process of learning. Curiosity and experimentation will be rewarded by video view stats. Rote learning will seem bizarre. We will stop making people 'bad' for not having uniform knowledge sets. Games will be ubiquitous. But most of all, learning will be social.

I can see the edge of it now, as my curious son quickly chases down online videos to learn about water rockets or caring for a pet mouse. Soon he will be posting his own experiments and entering into conversations with others on what works, what doesn't, and working in teams to do it better. We had craft and specialty magazines to tell us how to make things before, but now we have easier, cheaper access with the ability to talk with others as we create. The scale and social dimension offered by the internet together bring exponential expansion to self-directed learning.

Collective Markets: The Sharing Economy

The social revolution is perhaps most visible in the way it is transforming markets. Ownership may have been crucial in earlier times because it allowed someone to have more control, but no longer. Access now trumps ownership.

With a service like Zipcar, people can share cars with complete strangers because the trust is managed through tools and the service formatted like car-rental. Car-sharing services begin to move from rental-like operations to people sharing the cars they own – and not just for ride-sharing where the car-owner is driving – but for other forms of sharing.

Shared housing is also emerging as a new trend. Of course shared housing has existed for a long time, but now we have new ways of navigating the process that take shared housing to a new scale. Couchsurfing and airbnb make it easier to travel economically. For nomads tired of vanilla hotel rooms and wanting the comforts of home, the ability to find someone willing to lend a couch or rent a spare room makes travel more interesting and often more affordable than traditional hotels. At another economic class level, this manifests as house-swapping or renting vacation homes (often direct from the owner).

Share your movies, your vacation rental, your car. Share your experience and share your opinion. Share what you know. Share what you make. Some of this sharing has always existed in the gift economy. And, given the pressures of economic collapse combined with the technological ability the online world offers us, and supported by the development of stories of identity that focus on generosity and altruism, the sharing economy is expanding into the transactional realm.

Much like the impending shift in the political climate, the shift toward a more shareable economy seems inevitable. This bodes poorly for companies trying to convince people that they need more of the same object or experience. As more sharing happens, demand for first sale of product decreases. Instead, the life cycle of products becomes more valuable to consumers.

It will also be deeply disruptive to standard business thinking. Businesses will be challenged to shift their value proposition. If we are to move to

Sustainable Consumption, as Diane Osgood (Business Action Director for Sustainability at Virgin Unite and Senior Advisor to the Clinton Global Initiative) calls it, companies will need to think differently about why and how they produce what they do. Faster, cheaper, and more disposable will give way to full life-cycle design, closed-loop production, lifetime price and return rather than initial cost. Will we develop things like shareable warranties? Instead of dollar stores, will we have local barter-marts? And where do fab labs fit into sharing? On the upside, this bodes well for the environment as fewer used goods are tossed into landfills.

Sharing is also happening in the work context. Co-working has burst onto the scene and grown over the last decade. Whether it is a Jelly (where people co-work at a café or house) or a designated co-working space like the HUB network, sharing workspace offers a financial savings, stimulates creativity, builds better business networks, and gives legitimacy to start-up businesses.

A more contested area is intellectual property. Can I share a song that I bought with all my friends? If I have a paperback book, I can share it one friend at a time. If I have a digital copy, can I share it with all of them at once? Does my sharing take away from the rewards the creator and producer deserve? The manufacturer doesn't get any funds when I sell something at a garage sale or donate it to a good cause. Should the creator of a piece of intellectual property (like this book) continue to get revenue when the property is shared?

In a world of sharing, how can and will we reward the makers?

I haven't seen any good solutions to the intellectual property debate. The sharing economy seems fantastic in many regards, but it doesn't solve the age-old issue of how to reward the significant effort that people put into creating intangible, non-rival goods. Given the potential for real abundance and infinite sharing of intangible non-rival goods, our incentive system seems due for revision and no clear, compelling, and convincing answers have emerged yet on how to reward the makers financially.

Amanda Palmer wowed the crowd with her TED talk, 'The Art of Asking.' She has shown that artists can be supported for their creations even when the music is being shared freely. Just ask.

Looking again at how technologists address the issue – the usual business model is: develop the software and offer it for free; add a premium version; then do consulting and customization for a fee. Perhaps fee-based customization will ripple out.

In a world in which we co-create more and more in collaboration with others, mass customization as part of the expression of identity seems likely.

The Sharing Economy makes the new era of thriving highly visible. We can track much of it – what is getting shared through online channels. We can count the items and see the totals add up: eBay topples over $14 billion in sales/revenue in 2012. Etsy had $895 million in sales for 2012. Airbnb had estimated sales revenues of over $1.5 billion in 2012. This is visible. Before we couldn't really see what neighbors were sharing with each other or the vast secondary market of garage sales and flea markets. And with spaces like social media or the work of social business, it can be challenging to attribute hard numbers to this new way of being. The sharing economy is larger than all of the numbers you can gather on the various sharing economy companies, but it is at least the size of them: huge. The answer to our current financial challenges is not austerity, which freezes flows in the network. The solution to these challenges is the sharing economy where thrift leads to thriving.

Takeaway

The social revolution now under way permeates many domains of culture. It is most obvious in the field of communication with social media and what is now called trans-media. However, the cascading ripples from that shift in communication have implications for the way we conduct business, the way we invite and allow governments and other bodies and officials to govern us, how we learn, how we educate each other, and the policies and drivers around the infrastructure that the social revolution uses. We struggle in this new way of interacting at scale with each other. We question how to do it well. But we are learning and adapting quickly.

Innovative companies – from eBay to Amazon – are building platforms for small businesses to thrive. The line between who is inside and who is outside the organization is blurring. It is only possible to make this approach work, to pull disparate people together into effective, if temporary, groups and teams, if there is a clear, shared goal and a leaderless or champion approach. It would fail if we tried to do it from a hierarchical approach.

To run a great social organism, we need what Jim Collins calls level 5 leaders – people who are humble and exhibit a passionate professional will. Unlike the factory setting where a manager can watch the workers' hands at work, in this age – where design and ideas generate value – the manager can't witness the creative mind at work. People volunteer their minds to tasks that serve their personal purpose. People contribute their effort, led by an compelling idea.

A thrivable world is social and multi-pronged. It allows for extensive customization and significant redundancy (a strength in networks). Participation creates the sense (and fact) of agency and agency is acted out through participation. We each thrive where we have a sense of our agency and autonomy. We develop better processes for moving through the world together. And we are learning just how valuable our differences can be as diversity shifts from being a moral issue to a pragmatic one.

We do face some significant snags in the way of the unfolding new social realms:

- Monopolies – or near monopolies like Google, Facebook, and Amazon (with heavy political influence to maintain position: look at Bezos's purchase of The Washington Post) – have undue influence on our social technical infrastructure and are creating digital divides.

- reward and incentive system transformation for intellectual property (fixing this will unleash an unimaginable abundance of non-rival goods – a hundred-fold effect of the creation of Creative Commons licensing).

We continue to build our social technology and infrastructure to transcend these limitations. Of all the breakthroughs in the book, the two that seem most inevitable and game-changing are the shifts in governance and communication. The ripples from these two breakthroughs will impact most people and businesses around the world for a long time to come. And the pressure behind them is growing, significant, and unstoppable. So long as you're part of this emerging social reality (and not all of us are) the new era of thriving is inviting us to...

Level up!

CHAPTER 7

Metrics and Data Evolutions

Data may look like many things, but we rarely realize it is our mirror. The whole reason we accumulate data is to see ourselves more clearly. Data offers us a mirror to hold up to ourselves to see how we and our world are doing and to help us make intentional choices, even as a collective. We generate information to see ourselves, our actions, our impact, our world. If we ask "why do you want to see yourself/the world?" followed by a series of "why do you want that?" questions, we will tend to reach some simple answers: "because it inspires awe," "so we can take wiser action," "so we can change things for the better," "so we can put right injustice," "because we can act in greater harmony."

The old adage claims we get more of what we measure. Research certainly shows that we adjust our behavior based on the feedback we get through data, especially when that data is well presented in a timely manner.

This has spawned a whole movement in recent years for the quantified self where people can learn and share tools for tracking their behavior and health in order to alter their habits.

So, in what ways is our collecting and manipulating data a breakthrough? There are several parts to this answer. We have had breakthroughs across a whole spectrum of activity in this space: data collection, data formats, data openness and accessibility, data presentation/visualization, and data design.

Feedback Loops

Data – particularly visually represented data – is part of a feedback loop. It may be a positive self-reinforcing feedback loop or a negative feedback loop.

We assess where we are, use the data to shift awareness and garner advocates for shifts in action and policy.

I am talking about the kind of feedback loops that – once we've noticed them and measured them – facilitate change in the complex adaptive systems we participate in and generate. If we look at Donella Meadows' work on intervention points in systems, she listed feedback loops as #7 and #8. They are not the most potent ways of developing healthier systems, and yet they can be effective, especially when tied to #6 – access to information. Using data as part of a feedback loop and increasing who has access to, and understanding of, that data (by making it more accessible either through transparency or simplicity) also acts as an effective way of intervening in systems.

Where there is sufficient will and wisdom, we use data, visualization, and access to alter the rules of the system.

Having more data about community, environment, business, or collective health can help us add incentives, punishments, or constraints (which is #5 on Meadows' list of interventions). As we move toward a more thrivable world, in aggregate, the emerging new ways of collecting, sorting, displaying, and creating narrative around data can lead to a compelling shift in our goals for the systems we participate in. These goals can gradually shift, for example, from 'make more money and make more stuff for a more productive GDP; because whoever has the highest GDP wins' ... toward 'make people healthier, more autonomous, enabled to experience mastery, and charged with purpose; because whoever does that wins.'

Simon Kuznets developed GDP (gross domestic product) in 1934 to measure wartime production (he never intended to use it to measure wealth). And as we learn more about our world, we begin to see that we need new measures that better reflect the world we live in. Attempts to shift what we measure are already helping us know how healthy we are – these include Gross National Happiness, Progress Indicator, United Nations Human Development Index, Happy Planet Index, and many more. Each of these methods takes into account something that the GDP measure lacks, including levels of environmental destruction and human wellbeing, and disparities in financial wealth.

Additionally there are significant efforts to measure company wealth and health in more discerning ways than we did 30 years ago. Some of these have been in development for many years. Companies like Natural Logic help businesses develop metrics to demonstrate company claims about their environmental responsibility and help companies track progress toward goals of sustainability.

This has an enormous and cascading impact on our actions. And getting smarter and more effective at altering feedback loops is one more breakthrough that can lead us toward a more thrivable world. If we can see the effects of what we are doing earlier on, then solid data can help us advocate collective and individual behavior shifts, and it can help us track how much shift is happening. That said, behavior change can be hard – for individuals and groups – so it is important to be mindful that the data alone won't ensure shift. It is just one in our set of tools for altering systems and flows, but we are getting better at it very quickly.

Data Collection

The real and fairly quiet breakthrough in data collection is the sheer amount of computational power that we have access to compared to thirty years ago. We can collect vastly more data from more inputs from more sources than ever before because our systems of storage and processing allow it. And this can be done incredibly fast. Where we could once only hold up a mirror to ourselves once a year with the annual release of statistics, we can now often have real-time updating of data such as crime indicators or voting.

The more data that we can process faster the more we can see the data in relationship to itself over time.

The time element of the feedback loop is very important. As every parent knows, punishing a child too long after the event has little impact. The more closely you can tie the awareness of the result to the behavior, the more likely you are to get behavior change.

More important than the measurement of something, in many cases, is how measurements compare over time. Are we trending up or down? If we have earlier indicators of those trends, we can often soften the extreme ends of up and down, regulating the health of our systems.

Who collects the data is also changing. Take Ushahidi for example. Traditionally, the major news media and organizations such as the Red Cross collect and share information on deaths and other incidents in crisis zones. However, during the 2008 Kenyan elections and post-election chaos, people on the ground knew the media were not accurately reflecting the experience they had themselves. Ushahidi was born of this need and allows people to upload to a shared space what they have witnessed and where.

This generates a map of on-the-ground, citizen-reported data. Ushahidi has now been used around the world including during the crisis in Haiti. It has helped to organize rescue efforts and bring some transparency to crisis situations.

Who is collecting the data affects what data is collected, how it is presented, and thus what impact the information has. If governments or the news media are editing the information in order to skew public opinion, the ability of citizens to track their own experience and share it with others circumvents this kind of manipulation. We see this time and again with news hitting Twitter. Those on the ground during major events provide more information. There's no promise that the information is fact-checked, of course, but if enough people locally are saying it, en masse it becomes more reliable.

Thus, as people get control of their own information flows, they have greater power to make informed decisions about actions they want to take. A more thrivable world emerges when people have greater access to the information they need and have greater power collectively over the flows of that information. It increases our sense of autonomy and agency. It pushes power out to the edges rather than it being held by the few, who usually become motivated to maintain their power rather than seek the greater good of the people as a whole.

Data Formats

The kinds of data we collect and how we format it has also undergone a crucial shift. For example, 30 years ago when we looked at organizations, we drew organizational charts based on authority. Network Analysis, using surveys, collects information about who is interacting with whom, and then generates maps of relationships. We can now perceive better who has implicit control of information flows within organizations and networks. Social Network Analysis has also been used to understand the web of interrelations underlying terrorist groups, the housing crisis, academic references, social media, and lobbying of Congress.

When we can perceive the flows of money and information around us, we can make more informed decisions about voting, spending, and connecting.

Take a look at the Sunlight Foundation. They help organize information from a trans-partisan perspective. I worked briefly with Valdis Krebs on organizing social network data from a place like Sunlight to show who was lobbying Congress on healthcare issues. When you can see who is lining whose pockets, you can then check that against votes to see if corporations are indeed influencing politics. That sort of data being clearly shared can change the political game from several angles – lobbyists have to get more creative about the funding channels, creating more middlemen between funders and congress, sure. But also more fact-checked articles are available to the public about which politicians are being influenced by what lobbyists being paid by which corporations. Vote on! Places like the Sunlight Foundation can give you an API for that.

There can also be major leaps in efficiency. For example, putting data into consistent formats increases our ability to move the information around. This can be as simple as creating Customer Relationship Management systems that reduce the need for data to be entered and updated more than once. Organizational Knowledge Management helps to catalyze flows of knowledge and grow living organizational awareness.

Most of us are still stuck updating a dozen profiles online when we change jobs, locations, or other pertinent information. We are on the cusp of changing that too – so one change will cascade to all the locations where it is needed. A wiki database system such as wagn enables that within a single site (and is working towards making it possible across multiple iterations of wagns). OpenID and other cross-platform sign-ins are also making it more possible for updates to cascade across the web.

Many organizations are working on giving 'users' control over their data championed by Identity Commons and the Personal Data Ecosystem Consortium. To a small degree this functionality already exists in social media, with Twitter posts showing up in Facebook feeds. But imagine updating your LinkedIn profile and having it populate that data on your website, your work websites, and your social media portals. As this scales up, the ability to share the right nugget of information with the right people at the right time increases, enabling individuals and the groups they belong to see themselves and thus (possibly) act more intentionally. Additionally, such cascading changes through systemized formatting will save people time and effort.

Microformats is a coding effort, championed by Kevin Marks and Tantek Çelik, to scrape standardized data such as events (date, time, place, activity) from websites to aggregate them where other people might see them.

Formatting can also be about synthesizing information – what is the overall feel of a long text or collection of texts, for example? What is the collage of key words we can quickly scan? Tag Clouds help us grasp the key concepts in a large body of text. They count how many times each word is used, size each word in relation to the count, and arrange them in visually interesting (although not always informative) ways. In an age of information overload, ways of processing data that synthesize large chunks of it help us manage the overwhelm. Many of these new formats give us insight into patterns that can be found in larger bodies of information.

Data Openness and Accessibility

While we have this vast proliferation of data, it can only be of use to those who have access to it. A major revolution is under way in data openness and accessibility. Not only are we getting smarter about what data to collect, how to process it and format it, we are opening up and sharing that data in numerous new ways.

Of course, those who stand to lose from this information becoming more accessible are trying to resist this movement. Battles are being won and lost over this issue all the time (but mostly won). In most battles between spiders (representing brittle centralized power) and starfish (representing hydra-like decentralized power through network action) the starfish will eventually succeed. Data will become open and accessible.

To increase data portability, we need standardization of formats. For example, as new groups of city data are being released in large waves across the United States, there is an ongoing effort to standardize the data formats, so that data from one city can be read by an application designed for another city. Open data is not enough; it must be accessible as well. There is a significant movement of software developers striving to connect with government and business to make information about crime, transportation, politics, money flows, and other areas accessible to citizens and organizations.

Additionally, the data openness and accessibility movement is striving to make information about companies more accessible. For example, the recently launched GIIRS sets a standard for the social and environmental performance of companies and funds. And thus we see a movement from (1) high-profit investing – only seeking high-profit returns – to (2) socially responsible investing – which was more like screening out what you found unacceptable to invest in – now to (3) impact investing where you can invest with deeper knowledge about companies that are having a positive social and environmental impact.

When we invest for high profit, we can take the funds earned and put them toward making meaning in our lives. When we invest for impact, the meaning-making comes in the very act of investing; plus we can use the profits to create more meaning. On top of that, by affiliating with others who invest for meaning and purpose, we create connection and community, again enriching our lives – and increase our sense of individual and collective agency.

The pattern of increasing information flow to empower decision-making leads time and again to the core human needs for autonomy and purpose.

Data Presentation and Visualization

The increase in computational power also improves our ability to present and visualize information. We have been generating ways to visualize data for eons, and the last 50 years of computational breakthrough driven by technology mean we can gather growing amounts of data. We use data visualization to show relationships. The breakthroughs making a significant difference in our understanding in the last 15 years include programs like Gapminder which shows data over time tracking child mortality, lifespan, financial status, etc. by country.

These visualizations give us meaningful feedback and exemplify the dramatic evolution in, and increased access to, data presentation that started with Excel making it easy for just about anyone to produce pie charts linked directly to data.

A whole movement has been spawned, thanks in large part to the work of Edward Tufte and, at the edge of data visualization, there also exists the emerging field of data as art. We can also generate whimsical ways of knowing ourselves, as Jonathan Harris has done by capturing snippets of emotions and showing them in motion over time in 'We Feel Fine'. In 1998 I curated an exhibition entitled 'Text and Territory: Navigating Immigration and Dislocation'. In that exhibition, I included works from Julie Mehretu, whose work captured a diaspora on a geographical map. However, it was artistically rendered rather than data driven. Today we have artists like Maria Scileppi who make art direct from data.

We are even using visualization to capture meeting notes. A whole field of visual facilitation has opened up in the last decade where artists can capture the essence of a talk or conversation in notes so useful and captivating you would have done more homework if you'd had them in school! When data is presented in ways that appeal to us, help us understand ourselves, and tell a moving story, we engage powerfully and deeply.

The New Panopticon

There are risks associated with openness and accessibility, of course. Individual privacy and the right of corporations and governments to keep information secret continue to be strongly debated. A totally transparent world is a harsh one. Data is quite revealing and our media-airbrushed view of the world may look uncomfortably wrinkled when that data is revealed.

Additionally, questions about the indefinite retention of information online make forgiveness difficult. Should a 40-year-old be judged for the party pictures taken when she was 19? Should a company that makes an error, then acknowledges and corrects it, continue to be judged and even ostracized for the error? When do we allow forgiveness? Humans can forget and forgive. We aren't very good at it, but we can do it. Information systems do not. Should data have a shelf life? If so, which data and for how long?

Additionally, debates around online identity, who owns the data about us that exists online and fears of the panopticon (which describes the way 'they' can to see everything 'we' are doing), continue to be hashed out. Questions about identity that were once purely theoretical become of practical concern as data gets associated with people. Most recently the concern around real names on Google+ reveals how dangerous it can be to have a singular identity associated with a real name. The ability to use a pseudonym has been crucial in allowing what can't be spoken to be voiced, and in offering refuge to those who are stalked or otherwise being victimized. Additionally, it allows people who can't speak from their professional positions to participate in spaces they would otherwise be silenced in – by their very position. It remains unclear how this will be resolved, and it may be possible to evolve more sophisticated forms of identity as well as contextual ownership of information.

Much like the online social world needing an etiquette book, we are still figuring out what the right etiquette for handing data ought to be. However, if we continue to orient to human wellbeing – where we value the ability of individuals to have agency, be autonomous, work toward mastery, and align with others toward a shared purpose, then all of this data manipulation may play a significant role in the gamification of a thrivable world. We need the data to know that we are making progress in the game. We need to use the data to remind ourselves that we have the competence to make the next play (because we can know we succeeded at a similar move in the past). Let's be pragmatists about making a thriving world and build it – not only on dreams of a better future, but on reliable, properly gathered, and well formatted data.

Takeaway

The possibilities that the data revolution allows are significant. We have ever better feedback loops to help us adjust our lives, our organizations, and our society. We can use the data we generate to strongly advocate for the kind of world we want. With sufficient will, we can use the data we are gathering to change the rules of the system we operate within. The emerging ability to see ourselves more accurately is already transforming the landscape around us and transforming the way we behave in that landscape. As we seek to lead ever more integrated lives of higher integrity, we can invest in businesses that we know are not only avoiding causing social and environmental harm but actively trying to make a positive contribution to the world around them. Knowing more about the flows of information, power, and money in our politics, we can reduce corruption, reward behavior by public bodies that is generative and community-focused, censure behavior by public bodies that is self-serving and unproductive, increase political efficiencies, diminish the need for bureaucracy, and create the opportunity for a more engaged citizenry.

Behavior change can be hard. Data is not a guarantee of changes. It is one tool within our toolset. And the better we can get at collecting information, processing it, connecting it, and then producing sense-making visuals of it, the more data can help us drive the change we want to see around us. In the process, we get better at perceiving the flows of money, power, and influence, enabling us to make better decisions about voting, spending, and connecting.

While we are making breakthroughs to better ways to see ourselves, we face and will continue to face many challenges around what constitutes ethical information gathering, use, and sharing. Still, the general trend of data breakthroughs enables a more thrivable world.

Overall, there are four layers of improvement in our data flow, each of which increases our ability to see ourselves and make better choices. Of course, we still need to be mindful about how predictably irrational people are and be aware of the default choices people have. However, we can improve individual and organizational decision-making by:

∓ increasing access to information

∓ improving the formatting and display of that information

∓ improving our ability to share that information

∓ improving the way the information is synthesized to enable clear choices to be made.

Imagine these layers compounding. People get a sense of autonomy, mastery, and purpose by generating and using smarter data flows and visualizations. That makes a more thrivable world. And the system gets wiser about what it is doing – self-awareness achieved by looking into the data mirror increases our ability to create more opportunities for more people to experience autonomy, mastery, and purpose. Finally, systems are increasingly operating in real time and are becoming more responsive, saving time and energy that can then be devoted to other ways of improving human wellbeing. These are upward spirals of compounding impacts leading to a more thrivable world.

Level up!

Summary of Part II

I challenged you, at the beginning of Part II, to shift your beliefs about
how humans operate, how we come together, and how we use data to make
shifts. This was not an all or nothing challenge. I don't expect you suddenly
to agree with me about everything – or anything. As a coach I tend to
work with high-achieving people who keep striving harder for more. The
expectations are high. After seeing one of my clients make themselves feel
bad for not hitting their achievements, I changed my own expectations of
myself. I thought, "well here is how I have been for however long. If I make
a change, that is worth celebrating." I stopped trying to hit my goals and
just built on the momentum created by even a small movement in the right
direction (toward my goals). Later I would learn that a sense of momentum
is useful in behavior change according to B.J. Fogg. So, I challenged you.
You don't have to agree with my story. You can tell your own story about
it. And you can add to it other bits that you are aware of. Consider this a
prototype and build your own version.

All I am asking is that you hit the 'refresh' button on your models and see
what repopulates the field of your awareness. What do you know now?

In Part II, we started by exploring how irrational humans are. I updated
our stories about Darwin and Adam Smith, since their ideas are often mis-
applied. For thriving, the big takeaway from Darwin is that each part of
the ecosystem fits. So we can ask, when modelling after nature, where do
we fit? And where do those around us fit? I challenged you to update what
you know about our human wiring – to include that we are not just greedy
rational actors, but are also wired to connect and be helpful. I invited you
to play. To think positive – not in the sense of blind optimism, but in the
focus on possibility while acknowledging how it is right now. I invited you
to consider that most people are acting from positive intent. They may
not know the best ways to act on that intent, but if you act as if people
intend well, you are more likely to thrive and be compassionate in ways that
support their thriving. I suggested that happiness is an area we need to get
a lot more rational about – putting that slow thinking fore-brain to work on
the subject. I invited you to consider that a thriving world can emerge when

we tap into the full spectrum of our intelligence rather than valuing one type over another. And I said "it will take the celebration of the whole mind and the whole range of capabilities that humans have to face the challenges ahead." Let's use our awareness of how we work to make our world work.

We can't do it alone though; we can only make the world thrive together. So we looked in Chapter 6 at Social Revolutions. There are two axes on which the social world is unfolding anew. First, how we communicate through the internet has enabled a different scale of social interaction. It is making our business, government, and education more social. In some cases it is as if the 'invisible hand' finally has the strength to wallop organizations that put profit before customers, employees, society, or the environment. Second, how we go about communicating and connecting is changing. This ranges from how organizations are led (ideas matter more than charisma) to the group process we use to do the work at hand. We are learning, at a board level, the practical value of trust, diversity, and cooperation. I touched on network organisms and leaderless organizations, which are changing the business and political landscape. Network production, at the right scale and customization, far exceeds the efficiencies of factory production. In light of all of this, the sharing economy shows us how thrift becomes thriving, with 21st century organizations that facilitate sharing generating billions in revenues. We are social animals. And we are getting much better at it.

Playing the thriving game means we need better metrics. We see ourselves through the mirror of data. And we are getting better at that too. I invited you to consider how we are learning to design feedback for behavior change at every layer in every system. We get better at collecting the data, have more capacity to store and process the data, and have better ways of formatting it to share information where and when it is useful. Some say "data wants to be free." We can't quite ascribe that agency to it, but many people are working to make more of the right kinds of information open and accessible, while keeping your private data private and owned by you, to be shared as you decide to share it. There is a lot of anxiety about how we are developing a panopticon to view ourselves. Rather than adding to the fear, I invited you to live in the tension of individual privacy and collective evolution. Let us see ourselves as we are. But not so that we enable government to control and regulate us. Let us see ourselves so we can play the thriving game for ourselves and our world. Be an agent on your own thriving mission.

I know you are most likely not a game designer or a designer of vast social spaces. And yet, because I believe in this leaderless organism, I believe that if each of us designs what is around us, it will lead to a thriving world that works for all of us. It's my belief that we all have the tools and know-how and – with a few bits of knowledge about how humans really operate and thrive and how systems work and change – we can all make tweaks to the world around us. It's like being a Wikipedia editor, only each of us is editing the universe of human engagement. I don't know which pages you should edit. I don't know what those tweaks are for you. Take what you like from these chapters, mix that with what you know about your world, and go make a thriving game for yourself.

What I do know is that if we each tell a story of thriving, if we each show compassion to one another, and if we each choose to work responsibly with others, checking our data as we go along, we are the only thing that together will form the antibody to the convergent crisis we face. We are the emergent resolution to the world's wicked problems. Let's do it and…

Level up!

PART III: DOING

Ever have that sense that doing something is going to be hard? And then somehow you get started? Somehow in hindsight it was easy, and you wonder why you struggled with it? I imagine that taking action for a thrivable world might seem difficult. I asked you to examine your stories and your perspective. I pointed out how operating in a complex adaptive system is challenging and different from working with the simple system expectations we have grown used to. On top of that I gave you some information about what we know about how irrational people care, how socially connected we are in new ways, and some hints at the data (r)evolution we are in. I've made the bold claim that if we orient to thriving then together we will shift the world. But I haven't given much clarity about how you can do that. I'm going to do that now.

Over and over I have watched friends and clients succeed in some endeavor only to get overwhelmed by the new possibilities that emerge when they move, take a new job or start their own business, or get out of a relationship that wasn't healthy for them. There is this disorienting moment where there is too much new and not enough known. It might all be good stuff happening, but the amount of shift is too great. Like Emily Dickinson, "I Dwell in Possibility." Yet I admit that being in a practice of doing that is a challenge. My mother, ever wise, offered me a key to staying calm in that shift. She said the different dimensions of your life: work, family, home, etc. are like legs of the stool. Being solid in several of them allows you to shift one or two of the others. Since then, when I feel lost in too much transformation, I focus on what is staying the same – and that I can be comforted by. I might be changing my work, but I still have my home and family. Make a list of all the ways you and your work or community are already thriving. Rest in that before taking the actions to change what you want to improve.

Another useful strategy that has worked for me is to narrow the choice overload. Clarify what you want to shift and what boundaries you want to set for yourself. It is like looking at a menu at a Chinese restaurant where there is giant choice overload, and saying – I am only going to consider the vegetarian section. Qualify the realm of choice.

What I offer in Part III on Doing helps with the choice overwhelm of possible actions to take toward a more thriving life, work, and world. In Chapter 8 I offer some strategies for generating more creativity. Bring that creativity to making your own games in the world around you with advice in Chapter 9 that draws on the experience of leading game designers and behavior change researchers. Finally, Chapter 10 has a very flexible framework that makes all this complexity much easier to handle.

CHAPTER 8

Creativity

What do the breakthroughs we have been exploring – in how we see ourselves, in how we come together, and in how our brains actually operate – enable? And what do we need to do to take advantage of this new awareness of ourselves? To make the world thrive more, we will need to be very creative.

The human drive, at the very core, is to create. Which is lucky, because thriving relies on generativity and the ability to create what is needed when it is needed. So what does it take to create? While we may want a linear 'factory' process to generate creativity, we won't get one. There are, however, conditions that positively correlate to creativity. Conditions. Not a formula. This is about emergence and isn't linear or causal. It is something that we can increase the probability of rather than directly ensure. Creativity could happen without these conditions, but most of the time it happens with some of these conditions.

Create the conditions and you will improve your chances.

My offering here comes from conversations with Valdis Krebs and Steve Crandall as well as work with artists, creativity facilitators, and others.

Valdis approaches the subject as a social network analyst, watching for the characteristics of networks that give rise to creativity. Valdis has eyes that twinkle with curiosity. When we talk, we often walk while he takes pictures. I have the sense that he is constantly taking in information about the world, processing it, and testing it against what he already knows. His title of Chief Scientist at Orgnet.com fits him splendidly.

Of Steve Crandall, Pip Coburn of Coburn Ventures (an investment firm) says "he is one of those rare Bell Labs geniuses that when I was growing up people spoke of in hushed tones." Always dressed in a t-shirt and jeans, Steve looks like everyone's idea of a physicist – scruffy, bearded, clever. Steve has given significant attention to what gives rise to creativity and has deep experience creating innovations: creations that you likely use on a daily basis.

I have listened to their stories and this chapter is laced with insights from those stories.

Serendipity

Serendipity is the chance encounter, the chance connection of the previously unconnected. For more serendipity – increase the number of different experiences and people that you are exposed to. Expose yourself and your collaborators to new situations, ideas, contexts, and possibilities. Valdis talks about finding people who are different than you are. To the degree someone is the same as you, adding them to the conversation doesn't increase the possibilities. Seek out difference.

You need enough similarity to be able to connect and enough difference to bring something unknown or unexpected to each other.

Steve was explaining to me, after many conversations about creativity and innovation, that serendipity is not only the seemingly random connection of things in a meaningful way, it is also noticing that the connection is significant. Be mindful. Take the time to notice.

Look for the unexpected, the unusual, and then flip and find the unusual in the mundane.

What is so obvious that everyone overlooks it? Ask if it is significant._

Practice divergent thinking when you are seeking serendipity. Make long lists of all the different ways to see or use things. Generate lists of possibilities. Who else might you speak with? Get your nose out of your smart phone and notice the signs around you, the people around you.

Play

If it feels heavy, it will get attention from the conscious, linear thinking mind. Take the pressure off and play. Generate lots of wild ideas. Think of things that would make you laugh instead of worrying about what might actually work. Steve has this wonderful expression (borrowed from Douglas Adams): innovation is like throwing yourself at the ground over and over again until you finally miss the ground and start flying. If you take yourself too seriously in the act of throwing yourself at the ground, you won't take enough risks to generate something really creative. Instead you will try 100 small variations in a very methodical process. If you are afraid of hitting the ground, you won't really throw yourself at it. When brainstorming, keep your own inner critic in check to allow yourself to play with what might be possible.

Tickle the fear out of yourself and play with possibility and with your collaborators.

Engage in improv games. Say, "yes, and" not "yes, but" to other people's ideas and your own.

Steve tells stories of Friday creative jams at Bell Labs. He and several others would gather together. One – a catalyst – would listen and encourage them. They would go wild with the craziest things they could come up with. Then, later in the session, the catalyst would sort and summarize their best ideas. I call it a jam because, like jazz, it was each person knowing how to play with others and giving their best pieces in a space of play. They built on each other, jamming off the ideas of others to flesh out the barely imaginable. The vast majority of the ideas generated were tossed away. When Steve describes them, he is focused on how much fun they were and how creative they could be instead of what they led to. This is a sign of play – that the process is alive and enjoyable (even when challenging). Play takes the pressure off outcome.

Play is one of the best antidotes to fear. When my son was little, he would worry about the monsters that might come in the night. I told him if there were monsters, we would find them and tickle them! It turned his fear upside down. Not by diminishing it and suggesting he should be brave and 'manly' in the face of monsters. It diminished his fear because it took the fearful thing into a different context, turning it into laughter. Reading a bit of *Where the Wild Things Are* and watching *Monsters, Inc.* probably helped too.

Play is not just the making of a game, it is the playfulness that we bring to the game.

Randomness

The path to innovation is neither a straight line nor a clear flow chart. It is a jumble of odd experiences that a creative brain makes note of and creates meaning from. Creative people are ones who can take the random bits and make something from some of them. Encourage randomness. Flip a coin to decide what direction to take. Steve takes this coin flipping to astronomical levels. In graduate school, he and a friend would flip a coin to see what direction to take at any decision point in a drive. They made it from New York to Chicago before having to call home for money to get back. You never know where you might end up if you cultivate randomness some of the time. It might be a pleasant surprise and certainly will make for an adventure.

Steve talks about developing the idea for audio compression technology by trying to figure out how mother bats can find their babies in a cave of thousands. They screen out sounds other than the sound of their baby. From bats to audio compression is not a straight line.

As we just saw, serendipity plays an important part in creativity. A network poised for serendipity is more likely to generate creativity. Steve talks about how the buildings at Bell Labs were like a labyrinth. It was easy to get lost. People of different backgrounds were mixed together and chalkboards filled the halls. This encouraged random interactions between people with differences and tools for them to brainstorm together. Steve also says another creative organization he has worked with designed its building with centralized bathrooms to encourage interactions with unexpected people.

Randomness helps trigger serendipity, if we allow it.

Paradox

Seek out the tensions in paradox. In my explorations of thriving, I come again and again to apparent contradictions and paradoxes:

- Smart phones connect us to one another and to a world of possibility – but they disconnect us from our environment at the same time (which is why I was just urging you to get your nose out of your phone!).

- Doubt has underpinned human growth and development throughout history – it has led us to question and challenge old beliefs, assumptions, prejudices and dogmas and to find better answers. But doubt is also corrosive and can undermine everything we do.

So much of the talk about innovation seems to be about exploring something on the edge. But when you look closely at what these edges are, there is a paradox. Maybe you feel the brain tickles that come from paradox. So much humor comes from presenting us with seemingly opposing ideas in juxtaposition. Much art plays with this juxtaposition. Something ephemeral combined with something concrete: the photograph of a ballet dancer in flight or the gesture of an artist's emotion locked into canvas (Pollock). Something of high art mixed with something mundane: Andy Warhol's Campbell's Soup Cans or Duchamp's Urinal. The unfolding arises from the tensions inherent in paradox. When you want to be creative, consider how to fold opposites into one another. Find an axis of commonality and twist it – like those libertarians mingling with social justice advocates to form a new party based on individual autonomy and agency.

Trust and Safety

As a recovering control junkie, I was really struggling with these stories of randomness and serendipity. I realized that I just needed enough trust and safety to feel free to embrace play. Trust and safety act as the ground of creativity. If we don't have them, we can't try things. We resist change. We become afraid to fail or look silly. Our mind-time focuses on social dynamics instead of playing with ideas. If we happen to be in groups where trust is missing, the only course is to trust ourselves. But trust must be there. Part of my awe of Steve comes from recognizing that he has a different set of requirements for trust and safety than I do. Safety is important. Sure, I mean physical safety but I also mean things like financial safety. Hearing some of Steve's stories, I am amazed that he is still alive. But he is also someone that does not have a mortgage on his home. He carefully managed his money over decades so he can be free to play.

Know where you need safety and trust. It frees you up to play everywhere else.

Question everything… but not all at once… and not without trusting yourself to figure it out.

Be super clear what your boundaries really are. Where do you need to be safe? Where and what do you need to trust? Who do you rely on?

Deep Curiosity

I almost forgot this one because it seems so obvious. When I was in the humanities, I noticed that those most dedicated to their work shared a trait – a deep curiosity about some question or another. As I explored beyond the humanities, it still seemed to apply.

Curiosity is the fuel for exploration. It is what feeds us in a space of profound un-knowing – the vast realms of unmapped possibility. We ask "why?" And the asking leads deeper into the question. Steve says the best questions lead not to answers but to more and better questions. Only the deeply curious are willing to go there. John Hagel would call them Explorers. When you live in deep curiosity, you question every element of how something is. Just not all at once. There is a sense that everything is sacred and yet nothing is. So you hold several aspects of an idea stable. Say I want to be creative about making a chair. Maybe I hold stable the legs, seat, and relationship to table stable; then I question materials. Or I keep stable the relation it holds to table and floor, but I question what it means to be a seat. To generate a more thriving world, we need to thoroughly question our assumptions from this kind of deep curiosity.

Try it

- Take a walk today. Imagine you are on a treasure hunt. Find an orange object, a loud sound, a whirrrring noise, a pastel color, something round, something soft, something fragile, a strange smelling object, and something you imagine tastes divine. Reflect on your experience of seeking these items.

- Next time you are solving something, think of five other ways it could be solved.

- Talk with someone you have never spoken to before. OR Talk about something you have never spoken of before. OR Talk somewhere that you have never spoken before.

- Creativity has a million faces. What sort of faces does your creativity have? Try to draw them or take/find photos of them.

Thrivability is about life giving rise to more life. It is about increasing possibilities. Being creative is crucial to that. And, given the challenges we face in becoming more thrivable, it is only through deep and bold creativity that we will generate the unexpected and powerful solutions needed to transform the world we have into the world we want.

At times I grimace when I hear people say we need to innovate our way out of this 'mess' together. I grimace because that feels like throwing technology at the problem without paying attention to the wider context. Innovating is not the only thing we need to do. We also have to learn to work together better, acknowledge how we function, and continue to see ourselves better – all the understandings we looked at in Part II. We can't do one without the other. We can't keep going as we have been, assuming we will invent some amazing technology that will transform all our problems. And we can't just work together better with what we have. We need to be creative, resourceful, and always learning if we are to increase our ability to give back more than we consume.

And we'd better have fun doing it. A thrivable world will not emerge from rationing and sacrifice. We will not be motivated in sufficient numbers by what we need to avoid – especially given that the events we need to avoid involve risks in the distant future. To address the challenges the future brings to us, we need to engage in creativity and play, which delight us and bring out the best in us as we strive toward greatness together. Create the conditions for creativity and...

Level up!

Takeaway

Creating a more thriving world demands our creativity. We can't control or force creativity, but we can foster the conditions that make it more likely to emerge. We can open up to the chance of serendipity – not only by connecting disparate things, but by noticing when those connections are significant. We can find the unexpected surprise in the wilds and then flip and find the unusual in the mundane. We can play more, especially when we are clear about the trust and safety we need to hold things lightly.

Bringing things that have not been connected together or coming up with a new idea can be triggered by seeming randomness, so seeking out and embracing what appears random to us can help us be more creative.

Live and create in the tensions of seeming paradox. And perhaps most importantly, being deeply curious can help you be creative. The perseverance that comes with deep curiosity can take us to unexpected places and over the hurdles that block others from reaching an idea or possibility.

If we continue as we are, we will get more of the same things and the predictions will be accurate. To really disrupt the systems around us, we need to be powerfully and potently creative. And not just a few of us. I think we each need to be creative. I mean that at several levels. If being creative for you is breaking out the colored pencils or paints, then do so. Make some art. I believe the joy it brings you will feed your ability to take creative action elsewhere. Be creative in your work, even if that doesn't seem like a very creative place. Be creative in your relationships whether they are new or decades old. Let's bring playfulness to one another. That too will feed us in ways that I believe lead to thriving – your thriving, my thriving, and the world thriving. Step into the tensions of paradox – your wellbeing and the wellbeing of others (us and them dynamics) – and twist them so they align in a new way that can enhance you and others.

Your creativity doesn't need to be a grand master plan. Be where you are, unleash your creativity from this moment in this place. I invite you to trust the unfolding of that into the world in ways you can't possibly anticipate. And, like a black swan, I cannot anticipate it precisely either. I just know that over and over again I see it lead to unexpected generativity – and that it is something worth doing.

CHAPTER 9

Creating Together With Games

Creating mostly by ourselves may feel terrific. But, in organizations and in society at large, we create together. There is a whole spectrum of co-creation here. One friend of mine has been in a writing group where each person contributes three words at a time to a story. Steve Crandall can talk about co-creation of inventions. I curated the *Thrivability Sketch* as a co-creation with more than 65 other people. But look broader – our very culture is a co-creation. Our financial systems and economies result from co-creation.

It is one thing to bring a team together to co-create, but how do we intentionally co-create financial systems? Cultural practices? In many ways, it is about making games. It is an implicit game to act in the financial world. Education is also a game. Follow the rules, score well, and you win!

I try to make cleaning the house a game for my kids. Turn on the music, set the timer, and whoever cleans most or best wins a prize.

How do we make games more explicit? And how do we adjust the rules and rewards of the game to get the outcomes we want? Welcome to gamification and welcome back to the world of behavioral economics.

Gamification takes what we know about human behavior – as individuals or in groups – and develops metrics and feedback to guide us through a course of action.

In this process, we move from information collection to psychology. What motivates people? How do we influence behavior? Behavioral economics tells us that not all people are motivated by the same things. We share some traits but things quickly become complex as we learn that some people are motivated by a sense of achievement, some by a sense of power, and others by a sense of social connection. As we saw in Chapter 5, people are motivated by a sense of being a part of something larger than themselves – a sense of purpose. People function well when they have a sense of autonomy. And people strive for mastery over knowledge and actions aligned with their goals. So how do we design incentive systems that leverage these human dynamics? The field of game design has been working on these issues for many years, and it has come up with some effective solutions. Which is why there has recently been a burst of interest in gamification outside traditional gaming environments. How do we gamify a business? How do we gamify our social goals?

The practice is not new. Advertising and sales have long pursued psychological research on why people behave the way they do and what they respond to. The push to gamify the world is simply an extension of what we're doing already. Our first passes at this were fairly superficial with badges and leaderboards, but we are learning. The potential of intentionally tweaking the games we are already playing in business and government could lead to a very different world than the one we have.

Creating a thrivable world will require significant gamification. Rather than forcing people to move away from what we have – to sacrifice what they treasure and give up their current ways of living – we need to incentivize action toward the world we want. In a way, collecting data and visualizing it is already playing a game. The Millennium Development Goals were a very large-scale rudimentary game. As we continue to learn about game design in social systems, we get smarter and smarter about how to put the elements of the game together to stimulate the desired action in fun, engaging, even addictive, ways. What if co-creating a thrivable world became the most addictive game you ever played? One so fun you were playing it every waking hour? Together, we might win and...

Level up!

Zero-Sum Games and Non-Zero-Sum Games

Winning together sounds odd because we're used to zero-sum games. A crucial design element in games is whether they are zero-sum or not. A zero-sum game is one in which if I win, you must lose. We can't both win if we are on opposite sides. We tend, often, to think that all games have this quality. Non-zero-sum games are ones where, if I win, you win too. And if you lose, I also lose.

The idea comes from political and economic theory, and it means that, if wins are plusses and losses are minuses, the equation will end up with zero. Think about money. My friend Alfred, all English beer and unnamed tea, sweats with excitement. He's just cut his first trade and has come out to tell me about it. He's started a business selling widgets and he's found a supplier in Zeno. A kid who sleeps all the time and looks slightly gnomic, Zeno wears striped Osh Kosh overpants and he's looking mighty pleased as he's just made his first ten bucks. Here's how it went. They started with zero. Alfred borrowed $10 so he could buy the widgets from Zeno. Alfred gave Zeno the $10. Now Alfred has –$10 and Zeno has +$10, and the system has a zero sum.

While there are lots of games we play that actually add up numbers, such as football, in the end one team has more points than the other and therefore is the winner. What matters most is not how many points but who has more. This zero-sum game mentality shows up in our behaviors toward each other. Do we act as if my having something means you can't have it? It puts us in a competitive mindset, and we behave like opponents. Take any dualism and make them duel it out.

Where are there non-zero-sum games? Can we, as humans, transcend the competitive mindset and behave cooperatively? Are there games where helping you do well helps me do well? Sure, there are lots of places we interact where this is true. I play a lot of what I call gratitude games. I give thanks to people who are helping me or contributed to great conversations or insights. I tag the thank you with #gratitude. I have an infinite supply, in effect, of gratitude to give. Giving it doesn't diminish me in any way. And the person receiving the gratitude is also not diminished for receiving it. This works with other acknowledgements. Saying who has helped me develop a project has never diminished the credit I get for being involved in the project. Even a potluck could be seen as a non-zero sum game – everyone who comes contributes something to the meal. Sharing recipes is non-zero sum. I gain a great recipe and you get social credit with me for contributing to my wellbeing through the recipe. Lots of small community behavior fits in the non-zero-sum group.

Sitting in a farmhouse near Wabasha, Minnesota, I was told the story of farming "in the old days" by someone who had been there to participate. She spoke with a great deal of nostalgia about a time of sharing. During harvest, groups of farmers would travel from farm to farm helping bring in the harvest. The host farm of the day would provide the meal. They shared equipment and their time. This might seem a bit crazy since they were competing in the marketplace with the harvests they brought in, but they were all made more successful for having helped each other. Non zero-sum.

I have always been surprised that business plans have competitive analysis and yet don't adequately describe the cooperative network the organization will be embedded in.

Remember rival, non-rival and partially rival goods? Rival goods tend, predominantly, to be negotiated through zero-sum games. My having apples means you don't. But non-rival goods can be experienced much more easily through non-zero-sum games. If I develop that cookie recipe and then share it, I can have it and you can have it too. If you improve on it, and share your improvement with me, then we can both have the improved version. Open source software often takes advantage of this non-zero-sum-ness.

Non-zero-sum games also often apply to situations where we share a common good. If I take care of, and contribute to, the commons, then we can all partake in it. Same if you do. If however, I abuse it or damage it, then we all lose access to it.

Our outcomes are tied together.

Care for the environment and our infrastructural systems are non-zero-sum games. If any one of us doesn't care for them, then we reduce the ability of all of us to have access to them. Perhaps not in the short term. But it is a game we are all in together, to win or to lose as a whole.

Partially Rival Goods

Our models of the world have not been accurate enough and have resulted in some unintended and pretty dangerous consequences. If we focus on flows more than stocks, we notice this peculiar phenomenon of partially rival goods. Brett Frischmann introduced me to this concept. At the time Brett was a lawyer and professor in Chicago. Since then, he has released the book, *Infrastructure: The Social Value of Shared Resources.* He describes partially rival goods as those things that, with appropriate flow, can be experienced as if they are non-rival. Take driving down the highway, for example. If very few people are driving on the road when you are, it is as if the road is a non-rival good. You have it mostly to yourself. But if enough people use the road, congestion clogs it, making it into a rival good – I can have it but you can't. The discernment that he points out is a crucial one in understanding how to take action for a more thriving world. My takeaway from what Brett taught me about partially rival goods is that we need to play non-zero-sum games when we deal with them. This is at the heart of the work for which Elinor Ostrom shared the Nobel Prize in Economics – solving the tragedy of the commons. When we share a common good and we approach it as a non-zero sum game, we can work to prevent the common good experiencing 'congestion' and agree on how to navigate any congestion that arises. We need to behave differently with rival goods (like limited natural resources), and partially rival goods (like utilities, forests, and roads), as opposed to non-rival goods (music, books, recipes) if we are to move beyond the unintended consequences we have caused whenever we have treated any of these as if it were one of the others. How do we do that? By making new agreements for the games we are playing. (The whole Intellectual Property debate is a good example of this changing of the rules. An idea is a non-rival good that has been constrained into a rival good (IP) to ensure financial profitability. But there are other ways to handle the problem of how to reward the person who had the idea in the first place.)

Game Dynamics

Why are game dynamics important right now? Because they get people to do things easily and eagerly. Games use feedback loops to encourage desired behavior. They engage our emotions. They break down complex tasks into small steps. And they present triggers for action precisely when we have the ability and the motivation for that action.

This is based on the behavior model of Stanford University's Professor B.J. Fogg, which posits that the convergence of the following enables action:

- Motivation – wants to do it
- Ability – has the capacity to do it
- Trigger – is prompted to do it.

We have already explored the models for motivation proposed by Daniel Pink and Mihaly Csikszentmihalyi. Pink's model correlates well with Maslow's well-known hierarchy, where Purpose, Mastery, and Autonomy are seen as three elements of self-actualization.

These are like knobs and dials on the mixing board of game dynamics. It isn't that one is better or worse than another, it is that for any situation or game, one or more may be more appropriate and effective than another, especially for the specific target audience. And different players may often have different motivations.

When generating games, we need to explore the 'why' of people participating and the 'why' of each activity in the game.

In designing games, we need to consider the ability of the players. This can mean their physical or mental ability, but it could also mean the amount of time they have and their access to external resources.

Self-perception matters significantly here. It may be possible for people to play the games with the abilities they have, but if they don't believe they can, then they won't. Game designers can alter their perception of their abilities! And that builds up their sense of their ability to 'level up' too. Triggers complete the model and catalyze the desired behavior. What will prompt the player to take action? Prompts are based on motivations and abilities as well as reflecting the kind of player in the game. Think of this as the call to action.

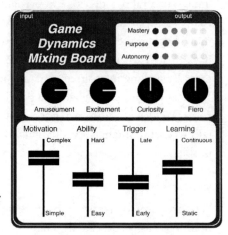

Game Dynamics Mixing Board

Getting back to the fun in games, Nicole Lazzaro of XEO Design, talks about the emotions in gaming. To the usual rational list of goals, actions, and motivations, she adds the magical element: emotions – because emotions create loops and glue the game together. We play the game to ride our emotions. It undergirds the whole thing. The rational layers are the building blocks of how to navigate the emotions that games can create. I found this particularly useful because of a key learning on decision-making:

Decisions are emotionally driven.

When people experience trauma to emotional centers in their brain, the rational/logical parts of their brain can get trapped in listing pros and cons endlessly. They can't choose! When our brains are working normally, it is an emotional reaction to the pros and cons that triggers action. Since I read about this, I have been keenly interested in how emotions guide behavior. You could say, I began to take emotions very seriously. Try watching all the decisions that get made in a day. Can you see the emotions at play behind them?

During her research in 2004 capturing facial expressions during game play, Lazzaro identified four emotional drivers (or four kinds of fun):

- ⊤ Amusement or People Fun – which is our social bonding
- ⊤ Excitement or Serious Fun – which is about meaning and value
- ⊤ Curiosity or Easy Fun – which is about imagination
- ⊤ Fiero or Hard Fun – which is about mastery.

If you think all this stuff is just 'fun and games' and not the serious stuff of remaking our world, watch out. Games are already being created to address significant real-world issues. For example, *Urgent Evoke* is a game developed for the World Bank Institute. Its website says: "The goal of the social network game is to help empower people all over the world to come up with creative solutions to our most urgent social problems."

This is not the first or only game for addressing real world issues. There is a whole movement and an associated event, Games for Change, which was founded in 2004. There are now events in Europe, Asia, Latin America, and North America. But whether it is called a game or not, we can see the game dynamics at play more broadly in the world.

The game design of sustainability acts as one of the major hurdles to success. Organizations whose goals tend to look like escalating lines on a boardroom chart don't reorient to a decreasing line or the stable sustainability flatline. Even resilience – mostly flat with some variation allowing it to return to flatlines – doesn't capture what organizations typically recognize as success. And the whole way we register 'winning' at sustainability is anything but compelling. The path to winning is grim – give up everything you do that is bad and make compromises on ways in which you have succeeded in driving costs out of your organization. Just imagine your favorite video game operating with those kinds of rules and objectives. How excited would you be to play?

But there are some innovative people in the space who have found ways to make better games for action toward sustainability. If I had a magic wand, I would send CSR, Sustainability, and social justice people to a six week game designer's workshop series. They would learn about their audience – what the incentives and goals for that audience are, where their triggers are, what language to use (a brief primer on Haidt's *Righteous Mind* would help), how to show them they have the capacity to take action, and tie it all up with the four keys to fun. That could unleash the kind of games that could disrupt the world as we know it and launch us clearly sailing into a more thriving world. So let's keep exploring what that looks like and...

Level up! <bing, sounds of score being tallied>

Data Design and Incentives

To manage game play, we collect data. We design the data to achieve our desired goals. We use data as a mirror in which we can see ourselves and encourage or discourage certain behavior. And the data creates incentives. Along the way we need to ask these questions:

- ⊤ Why are we collecting data and what do we want it to do?

- ⊤ What goals are we trying to reach?

- ⊤ How do we use data to help us measure our activity in the pursuit of these goals?

Let's take a little dive down into the design of incentives. By incentive I mean the object, state, or experience we are striving to have.

If the object or experience triggers action, it is an incentive to a flow of behavior.

Personally I was drawn into games after having explored an expanded concept of currency. I was looking beyond alternative currency, at the very root idea of a current – or flow – and what triggers action for flows, with the Metacurrency founder, Arthur Brock. When I began exploring games and gamification, I saw the powerful overlap. Designing money is designing a game. We can design games at large or small scale to encourage the behaviors we all want for ourselves and in our communities. It was, of course, odd to note that the gamers had a much more developed sense than the currency designers of human motivation and what it takes to engage people in games. Many of the currency designers came at the issue from a 'problem and policy' point of view rather than from a pragmatic perspective – 'where are people and how do they actually work so I can design a system around their programming?'

Here are some types of incentive with examples of each.

- ⊤ **Medium of Exchange**: tickets, stamps, coupons

- ⊤ **Store of Value**: gold, assets, coins, airline miles

∓   **Metric or Measure**: page views, people served, ROI

∓   **Unit of Account**: number of packages, total shipped or sold

∓   **Performance**: time, strength, quality, grade, rating

∓   **Placement**: medal, title, level, leaderboard

∓   **Token of Status/Reputation**: degree, certification, badge.

Often, when designing an incentive system or game, we create a collection of incentives that interact with each other. Say we are playing the game of education. The culminating incentive might be the degree. How do we let people know they are making progress toward their degree? We give them credits for the classes taken toward the degree. How do we let people know how they are doing in the classes that they get credits for? We do we give them grades. How to we give them grades? We rate them on their performance, we count their attendance, we measure their progress through the material for the class. Systems don't often have a single incentive, they have a whole interdependent set of incentives that form the game. I just explained the student incentive elements for American universities. A different set of incentives motivates the professors, both within their school and within the broader space of academia. And universities are also acting on a set of incentives (rating, count of students, leaderboards, certification, not to mention the money flows).

In creating games for a more thrivable world, we need the right blend of interdependent incentives. We are already responding to incentives in almost everything we do. How do we want to alter those to get results we desire?

Try it

Whether you're in a position to incentivise different behavior in a corporation, a school, a family, or simply in your own life, it's interesting to explore the dimensions in an incentive. Reflect on how the following questions are answered by a token or incentive in your environment.

∓   Goal
    What is the goal it addresses?
    How do you know it is achieving that goal (or not)?
    What ways do you measure the system?

╤ Issuance

Where does it come from?

How does it enter the space?

What criteria must be met?

How is it tracked?

What gets recorded and is that part of the memory?

╤ Movement

Does it move after being issued?

If so how and under what conditions?

What permissions are given and who has agency in that interaction?

What are the rules of play? (can it go negative – less than zero? – how are disputes mediated?)

╤ Redemption

Does it get converted into something or redeemed?

If so, for what? under what conditions? by whom? and what governs that?

╤ Interaction

How does it interact with other incentives?

What is the relationship of value from one to the other?

╤ Closing

Does it get pulled from circulation? how? when? and why?

╤ Tracking

How is accounting done?

Who is it visible to? And who performs it?

╤ Governance

How does the system discourage being gamed?

Is the system self-organizing/learning or is it hard-wired?

What happens when it breaks?

How is trust in the incentive ensured?

Takeaway

To co-create a thrivable world, we need to leverage personal psychology to work together in a shared learning system where we can be creative and continue to evolve. Games can balance the dynamics between personal motivation and social action and use feedback mechanisms to improve play. You might be used to the competition of zero-sum games, but there are some crucial non-zero sum games afoot where you will only win if we win together – the environment, our shared infrastructure, our personal thriving as connected beings. In these non-zero sum game spaces there are often partially rival goods that need cooperative care to stay in states of flow – roads, public spaces, the commons, the internet.

Let go of the fascination with competition at work. Look in your organization for where cooperation is helping you to thrive. Our outcomes are entangled together.

The path to a breakthrough future is to be creative and innovative together, using games with their underlying feedback mechanisms tied to real-world data. Be clear in your personal or organizational game design about your motivation, triggers, and capacity. Remember that your decisions are emotionally driven. So learn the four keys to fun to trigger emotions for compelling game play. Design your data collection as part of your game. But don't take it all too seriously!

I am reminded, again, to be playful – it gets you to the big win faster :)

 @NicoleLazzaro
Nicole Lazzaro

The bigger the fear, the bigger the opportunity. The bigger the frustration, the more epic the win! #pxd

4 Dec 10 via Twitter for iPhone ☆ Favorite ↻ Retweet ↩ Reply

In gaming, an epic win is a success so incredible it wasn't believed possible until it was accomplished. A thriving world is the ultimate Epic Win. Let's go for it! As Nicole would say \o/ Game On!

CHAPTER 10

Action Spectrum

I am an action-oriented person. I am pragmatic. I want to know and understand things that matter. And things matter to me when they have some use. Pragmatic knowledge leads to wise practical action. Exploring uncertainty, system and network dynamics, and emergence has helped me understand what happens around me. And what do I do with that? I want to make more informed decisions and take wiser action. This led me to develop the Action Spectrum model.

This framework emerged from conversations with Herman Wagter, a theoretical physicist turned systems entrepreneur in The Netherlands. Herman and I meet in Amsterdam, London, and Paris for dinner or coffee to grapple together with how get systems unstuck. He has that quiet humble kind of brilliance that comes from long spells of listening to lots of different perspectives, playing with paradoxes, and the confidence that comes from repeatedly discovering 'magic bullets' that transforms a system. He has been using this framework over the last several years since we developed it. He uses it to pull together an ecosystem around supply chains or commons resources like transportation ports.

While I have no formal physics background, I often find myself engaging in conversations with physicists. My story about this is that physicists are willing to ask deep and probing questions in search of better questions. So many people get stuck in a story they want to have about the world. But physicists, as I have experienced them, question down to the most elemental subatomic level how the world works and what story we weave about it. Physics metaphors sparkle in most of the frameworks I develop. Physics is where math goes to play itself out in practice. And the Action Spectrum might be where thrivability agents go to make decisions and take action in a complex adaptive world.

We have to be careful when we take on a metaphor – the way the idea operates in one context (physics) may not translate fully to a new context (biology). Let's hold the metaphor lightly as we play it out. First, let's look at a root issue in physics: causation and its limits.

Limits to Causation

An important takeaway from the limits of reductionism (which we looked at in Chapter 4) – as well as understanding the distinctions between simple, complicated, complex and chaotic systems – is a way of seeing causation. In simple systems A leads to B. Without A there is no B. There is a real sense of control. I turn the ignition in the car, and it starts.

In complex and complex adaptive systems, there is not the same clear sense of causation and thus there is a feeling of uncertainty about control. In simple systems it is easy to ascertain why B happened. B happens because of A. In complex systems, B happens when certain conditions are met. These might include the presence of A, but there might be other ways for B to happen. We can find probabilistic or correlative connections. We can suggest a correlation although we might not be able to grasp why it exists. (Wave hello to quantum entanglement – where things can be correlated in ways we typically don't consider part of causal chains. Let's admit that physics has yet to accommodate for time being directional, which causality is dependent on. So claiming any causality might be slippery.)

Selling, for example, is often probabilistic rather than causal. Control is uncertain – we can't control the buyer, but we know that when we do certain things we are more successful more of the time in terms of selling our product. Good salespeople have learned the conditions for making sales and try to achieve them as often as possible. They have not done it by becoming more controlling of buyers.

Making friends is similar – we can be nice to everyone, but some people will become friends and others will not. We can't control it. Social media is very much a probabilistic phenomenon. Results are not guaranteed.

The same is true for creativity and innovation. To be creative is not a linear process: you cannot do A and C in order to be creative. It is about getting the right conditions for creativity to emerge. It can be fostered by certain activities, increasing the chances that a useful creation will, in its turn, emerge.

Whenever we are engaging in spaces where there is free will (and we can't buy agreement), we enter into complex – and often complex adaptive – systems.

In such situations, it becomes much harder to be clear about causation. We may think we can do simple experiments where there are controlled elements as if we were in a laboratory. But if we are in complex adaptive systems, we can be facing numerous interdependencies – where we can't just change one thing because, when we do, the rest doesn't stay the same. That doesn't mean we can't experiment – in fact it is all we *can* do. It just means we can't control for single factors. And we can't anticipate the same results when we think we might be conducting the same experiment. We can't locate the cause of what happens very well. We can only look for correlation.

But our tendency is often to create stories about causation, as if nothing in our lives happened without our controlling it. The dark side of causation we call blame. Tree Bressen facilitates cohousing groups. I was visiting with her to discuss group process. I noticed a wheel on her refrigerator. It had each member of the house, the president, the pets, and the weather. I asked about it. She said it was a 'Wheel of Blame' the house used whenever someone got upset. Let's say the dishes were not done. The one angry about the dishes being dirty would be asked to spin the wheel. Wherever the spinner landed could be blamed for the dirty dishes. The president? The weather? The dog? It brought some levity to the usual blame games people play. I would love to see an app for that! We can also use the giggle antidote to frustration when we want to blame someone.

In the same way, we often take responsibility or ask others to be responsible in systems they can't control. Maybe they can exert some influence, guide outcomes, offer nurture or support, but they can't control the outcomes. And we may also give individuals credit – that sense of sole creation or authorship – when what has happened is often a synthesis of ideas or actions, tipping points, collaboration, and always the 'standing on the shoulders of giants' phenomenon.

This is why Academy Awards' acceptance speeches come with a fanfare of thanking the many people who made it possible. We know it takes a crowd to make things. But, in far too many instances we forget this – and simplify things by valuing the most recent event and the lead individual, forgetting about the rest of the process.

How can we assign blame when we can't show cause? How do we measure and reward our impact when whole systems are involved in production? These questions are being asked right now in Human Resource departments, by foundations, investors, and many others.

157

Operating in a world of complexity requires us to navigate uncertainty without resorting to control and linear causation.

Even saying that oversimplifies things, because usually there are some aspects that involve control, certainty, and simple systems; and, at the same time, complex adaptive systems get entangled too. How then do we operate, given that direct causation is not as simple as we would like? It is not a clean and tidy story.

In direct causal systems, we exert control. In the activities where we can influence outcomes, we guide as best we can. With probabilistic entanglements, we feed the systems that we depend on – the way a farmer plants seeds and cares for the crops – even when we have no way of being sure, in advance, what our activities there will produce. That brings us to the Action Spectrum.

The Action Spectrum Model

In a reductionist world, we try to move as much as we can into the domain of our control. Thus ownership is vital. So is authorship. In the era that is unfolding, control will still be important, but we have learned the limits of control as well. We are beginning to grasp how important and valuable are the things we do in the space where we can 'only' guide and nurture. And we find that we can't privatize those spaces and activities.

However, this also confounds us. If I contribute resources to an infrastructure that I don't control, how will I know if I am getting a return on that investment? If I put money into social media activity, what can I be assured of getting back? How will I know if that money is well spent? We can generate some metrics, but the real benefits (and possibly the costs) extend far beyond that which we can measure or track.

The simplest story that I think demonstrates this is the use of a camera.

Control: You can control the camera. You adjust the lens. You

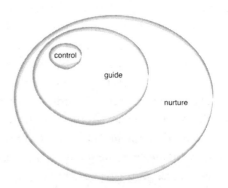

Action Spectrum
Portions of the system we can control, guide, and nurture

select the view. You hit the button triggering a predictable set of actions inside the camera that result in a photograph.

Guide: You take a picture of Jheri. She is funny. She sticks her tongue out just as you snap the picture. You might have been able to guide her ("can you stand next to that rosebush, Jheri"). You might control how much you zoom in on her, but you can't control her. And maybe that is part of the magic of the photograph.

Nurture: You post the photograph to Instagram and 10 times as many people see it and like it compared to yesterday's photographs.

What happened? Can we say that it was viewed more because of her tongue sticking out? Or because of her social network? Or because the #tongueout tag was trending that day?

The result of what you can control can be clearly attributed to you and what you caused to happen. It is obvious and fairly objective too. You took the picture. Snap. Photo. Done. The guide is getting a bit confusing. Is it your picture or hers? Who gets credit? (or blame?) It is created between you and Jheri – in your interaction. Can I really hold you accountable for controlling her tongue? The result of the photo being seen by so many people – can we attribute that to your fantastic skill with the camera? to Jheri's silly tongue? or to something else entirely – maybe even something we aren't giving attention to and that is beyond our control (#tongueout was the tag for a photo competition that day that we didn't know about). You try to reproduce the success with this photo on Instagram. Maybe now more people are following you, which changes the results. Or maybe you post it on a rainy day when everyone is hovering over their devices. You plant the seeds for the same success over and over getting different results over time. Your own version of A/B testing. Looking at the results of 50 attempts might let you know that you have a roughly 10% success rate, but it might take 10,000 attempts to find some patterns that often (though not always) lead to 'Jheri #tongueout' success levels.

Working with the Action Spectrum has been a very thorny issue in philanthropy. (I'll use philanthropy as an example for the rest of this section. But the Action Spectrum applies in all organizations and systems – you can apply it in government, in a school, in a restaurant, in a family, in a garden.) Donors and foundations want to know if their donations are creating the benefit that they intended. Yes, we can measure various ways in which a community might be improving. But we can't be sure it was a specific program that changed it. Maybe it was a larger economic shift. Perhaps it was a cultural evolution. And while we can factor out many of the possible causes with comparative studies, we are still uncertain. The causal connections are not clear and direct. We have to handle these uncertainties as we handle risk in investment portfolios. Some of us will need a lot of certainty and control to feel safe, others will leap out to the edge, believing that some of the seeds they nurture will produce the results they seek. The trouble is, the certainty of the control realm tends to correlate to the direct service forms of charity. We can count how many homeless people we fed today. It does not tend to capture the transformational change efforts very well. If I have a program that prevents 99% of kids from being homeless in their lifetimes... I am going to have to collect data for their entire lifetimes and I am going to have to show that homelessness was likely to have been a given rate, and that it was my intervention that changed that rate (and only my intervention really). Preventing disaster is not a glamorous business. No one can be sure you stopped something from happening. The glamor only gets glommed onto when the disaster is so clearly looming as to appear unavoidable. Then you get to be a hero. Read your comic books and see if this bears out.

So how can we perceive this full spectrum of actions and attribute agency in each of them appropriately? We need to have a 'portfolio of activity' and the right portfolio for me must correspond to my willingness to tolerate risk or to my organization's willingness to tolerate risk.

The chart that follows (General Principles) maps the basics of the Action Spectrum framework. It also explains what organizations tend to focus on in each of the three main forms of intervention. For example, to exert control over a system, organizations will place boundaries around it, claiming ownership over that territory. Organizational offices are one way of putting a boundary between what lies inside and outside the organization – so that the organization can then claim to control what happens within the boundary. It can then set clear expectations of what happens in that controlled area. In spaces where they can guide, organizations give attention to gaining cooperation from others that have influence over the outcome. Legal departments are often dedicated to this act of gaining cooperation (and minimizing the risks of that cooperation). And in nurture spaces, organizations offer rewards for their desired goals, coaxing some to respond. The XPRIZE Foundation, which designs and runs competitions for technological innovation, offers a good example.

Control	Guide	Nurture
General Principles		
Closed, simple systems Predictable consequences Mechanistic Reductionism works Short timeframes and quick feedback loops Organizations focus on: • placing boundaries • claiming ownership • setting clear expectations	Complicated, even complex, systems Attribution shared Organizations focus on: • incentives & bonuses for employees to cooperate • legal agreements Action success depends partly on interpersonal dynamics If the result does not happen, leverage influence or increase 'buy-in' of parties Effectiveness comes from improving the process and human dynamics	Complex adaptive systems Probability instead of causality Organic learning Attribution distributed Long timeframes with webbed feedback loops. (Warning: power laws live here.) Organizations focus on: • interactions that invite/ incentivize • encouraging innovation & creativity Same action produces different results Sow seeds and see what grows fruit Improvement unpredictable Iterate and watch for patterns

When we look at metrics across the Action Spectrum, we see that they change too. Metrics in the control space can be very clear and tangible. We know when the system works. We know, when it breaks, why it isn't working any more. Metrics in the guide space, as causality ceases to be as clear, also start to get fuzzy. We can see if the goal is being reached, even if we can't see what caused the goal to be reached. Say, for example, sales. I can count how many items were sold. I can't be sure why they sold. Was it the advertising? Was it the salesperson? Was it word of mouth? Better ask the buyer, even if the answer we get is slippery.

Control	Guide	Nurture
Metrics		
Measurable, countable Clear relation of input to output Dependable, predictable Zero-sum Examples: # of parts/ products, amount of money, length of video, rate of production	Milestone or goal achieved May be sortable or rate-able May be unclear what inputs were necessary to achieve outcome May be non-zero sum Examples: # of takes in shooting a film, rating of quality in the product, sales numbers	Sampling of outcomes (full measure unknown) Complex and often multi-layered metrics pointing toward intended outcome but are rarely the outcome itself Challenging to predict Wide variations Examples: eyeball or viewer count within time period, story attributing credit, change/deviation from previous measure

We can usually still sort the results – which are better and which are worse. We struggle to develop more complicated metrics to match the complexity of the system involved. Usually we end up defaulting to control metrics and pretending causality. We try for example to assume that the rating agency is some objective observer that was not influenced unduly and we forget to consider that their rating might be a comparison with others. We might have done better this year and deserve a higher rating, but everyone else also did better, so our rating stayed the same.

In nurture spaces, the metrics are very tricky. We just can't gather enough data to get the whole picture, especially in a short period of time. So we look for indicators of value. We take samples. We look for stories that attribute cause when we can't get quantitative information about our role in the result. Our organization just gave gym membership to our employees because physical activity is associated with (positively correlated to) both higher productivity and decreased insurance costs. We might be able to show that we did have fewer insurance claims or that our productivity increased (more products made or sold). But was it because of the gym or economic factors or that inspiring new CEO? And was the ratio of cost benefit the right one for our organization?

Control	Guide	Nurture
Benefits		
Excellence of what is known Known and clear agent or authority Predictable outcomes Easily measurable results	Share responsibility and knowledge Flexible, more resilient than control Shared attribution Guessable (not predictable) outcomes When guiding by shared values and principles, the system is self-managing	Agile Resilient, at times even anti-fragile Power laws Large-scale collective impact

While the metrics of the nurture space may frustrate us as we strive to know what impact we're having, it is still one that offers great benefits – it is agile, resilient, even anti-fragile. It is a space where power laws can be possible. The guide space has the benefits of collaboration: tapping into more wisdom, flexibility, and, when well designed, it can be self-managing. And we know the benefits of the control space: it is the known with predictable outcomes and easily measurable results.

Control	Guide	Nurture
Risks		
Monoculture Brittle, non-learning Tendency to stay small as effort needed to 'control' grows exponentially with growth in size.	Dependency on others Requires interpersonal skills (non-rational environment) Managers may resort to prescribing behavior, then things collapse Challenging metrics and more complicated feedback loops	Dependency on networks and others beyond influence Diffuse authority and difficult attribution. Unpredictable timeframes Uncertainty

With the benefits of each realm come the entangled risks. The control space is brittle because it's a monoculture and the opportunities for growth are limited. Think of *Encyclopedia Britannica* trying to compete with Wikipedia! The Guide space has risks too – there is dependency on others which requires interpersonal skills. And changing the behavior in the guide space challenges us because we are less sure what causes what to happen. The Nurture space is riddled with risks – network dependencies, hard to manipulate with nonlinear timelines. It is filled with uncertainty. Those who navigate the nurture space well often seem to set their expectations low – as if most efforts will fail but with the hope that a random few will be wildly successful. Think of the 'angel investor' approach. Many new business models are aimed at the nurture space: create a field where others can strive with their own small business. Amazon offers a space for sellers. Airbnb lets people rent their homes. The 'platform' business lives on small margins across thousands of small players where the risk of any single one failing can be compensated for by numerous others that survive.

We can look further into this model to analyze opportunities and potential impacts, and the forms of authority that operate in each space or type of intervention – you'll find more of this table online at triarchypress. net/thrivability. But let's take one simple example. Let's say I want to address homelessness, what might a portfolio of activity look like? As an organization my mission is to "end homelessness" and my lead donors are asking for me to demonstrate that I am making progress toward the mission.

I look at options like those listed in the table below and generate a scheme to say that for every $10 we take in, $4 feeds a homeless person a meal, $3 supports our program to work with at-risk youth on career and skill development, and $3 goes to educating the public about the root causes of homelessness and how we can all be involved. Then we ask our major donors to work with us on matching each $10 gift to support our operational costs to deliver these three programs. Then we create metrics across the space of each program. How many were fed? When we feed them we run a survey providing information about how they became homeless. We use that survey information to adjust our guide program working with at-risk youth and show that connection to our donors. Finally, we capture video of what we are doing and inspiring stories about people who were once homeless and are now successful. We show our donors how many people are seeing these videos and provide stories from people who reach out to us as a result.

Control	Guide	Nurture
Portfolio of activity for addressing homelessness		
Donate $10 to feeding the homeless Buy a newspaper sold by a homeless person	Attend city council meeting and advocate programs addressing homelessness Volunteer with at-risk youth to build their career skills	Invite people to the cause by sharing a well designed, emotionally compelling video on the issue Use your professional skills to work with an organization dedicated to the cause Fund a small group of homeless people to start a nonprofit or social enterprise

Whether you work with nonprofits or for-profits, showing your work across the spectrum can help strengthen your work and set appropriate expectations for each decision and action you take. There is a saying that happiness is equal to actual state minus expecations. It rings true... set appropriate expectations for each layer of the Action Spectrum activities to have happier and more productive organizations and people.

When I look out at what our current challenges seem to be, I conclude repeatedly that it is a result of mismanaged expectations about what form of system we are operating in leading to poor decision-making and actions. Thus, I invite you to use the Action Spectrum as a simple framework for making more system appropriate decisions and the actions that stem from those decisions.

How will you use the Action Spectrum to level up the way you play your games?

Try it

⊤ Draw three concentric circles, like the Action Spectrum diagram early in this chapter. Fill in each layer of the circles with decisions or actions you take.

╤   On a new sheet, try it for organizations you are affiliated with.

╤   Under the circles, consider how you design your metrics and the
     data you collect to support the actions in the three different areas.

Takeaway

Taking wise action in the world requires us to understand what we
can control and what we can't. But just because we can't control for
outcomes in all situations doesn't mean we can't take action. We can
guide, influence, nurture, and encourage. But we can't have the same
expectations from these actions that we have of the things we can control.

The thrivable world that is emerging now unfolds from this spectrum
of action – on an individual, group, community, and organizational level
and on larger, collective levels. How will you adjust your 'portfolio of
activity' having considered the Action Spectrum? Where do you know
you need to have more control? Where can you let go of your need
to control in order to nurture something larger than yourself or your
organization? Where are you working with others to guide each other to
mutually beneficial outcomes? How might you adjust your approach to
metrics across the spectrum?

Moving forward wisely means we understand better where authority
functions (and where it doesn't). Navigating the uncertainties before us
happens best when we embrace the qualities of the levels of the system
we function at.

A thriving complex adaptive world emerges from all of us controlling
what is closest to us and nurturing the spaces we share together.

Summary of Part III

I invited you, at the beginning of Part III, to consider where you wanted to take action and what you would hold the same. I shared how trying to change everything at once makes us lose our balance. Then I provided options to consider when taking action. In Chapter 8, I asked if you want to be more creative, how you could generate more randomness and serendipity. Play more. Tap into your deep curiosity and wrestle with the tensions of paradox. But ground yourself and your work in trust and safety, because without them it is difficult to bring the lightness of play to your creativity.

I argued that disrupting the systems around us to breakthrough to the thrivable world that is unfolding requires potent creativity from all of us. In big and small ways – we need to be creative in our own lives for the joy and lightness it can bring us which will infuse other areas of our lives with more playfulness. We need to be creative in our work, examining why a process works the way that it does and if it could be improved in ways that increase thriving and generate more value. I invited you to put faith in human ingenuity.

In Chapter 9 I offered some of the basic tools of games, building on what we have learned about personal psychology and motivation, to help design simple feedback systems that encourage the flows we want to have in our lives and work. I also made a distinction between zero-sum games and the non-zero sum games that we are all in together. By using motivation, a sense of capacity, and appropriate triggers along with the four keys for fun we can shape and shift our games to make the creation of a thriving world the most addictive game yet! Let's go for an epic win!

Finally, in Chapter 10, I offered the Action Spectrum framework as a simple tool to help each of us take practical action within the context of the complexity we explored in Chapter 4. What do you control? What do you guide? And what do you nurture? We need to manage appropriate expectations for each tier of the spectrum. We need to design metrics for the risks and expectations that fit each tier. We need to align our data collection activities to support the metrics we need to keep flow going at each level of the Action Spectrum.

As humans, we have a fundamental drive to be generative and creative – to generate and to create. As we evolve, there is a pull to adjacent possibilities and a pull outward as we expand both our creativity and our ability to track and make order out of the chaos of choice. A thrivable world demands significant innovation and creativity in the use of resources, the sharing of the environment and those resources, and the coming together to do something great. Epic, in fact.

It is a complex adaptive world out there. I hear lots of debates between doers and talkers. The trick is that taking action that isn't informed by experience and experiment too often turns out to be foolish (unless the system is chaotic, in which it is the only option, of course)! But talking about how we can break complex adaptive systems down into simple mechanical ones is just as dangerous. I invite you to join me as a pragmatist who values wisdom and experience and who is prepared to take bold, courageous action. Let's make a game, using the Action Spectrum framework, so that our lives, our organizations, and our world thrives!

You may have noticed that I slipped the term 'thrivability agent' into the last chapter. It's my belief that we need conscious, deliberate, slow-thinking, as well as better heuristics for fast thinking... that we need generous, trusting, compassionate, creative action if we are to rise to the challenges presented by a world in convergent crisis of breakdowns. So too, if we are to seize the possibilities presented by the insights and breakthroughs we've been considering. I think of people who are learning to act in that way as thrivability agents. I see myself as a thrivability agent. Please join me and...

Level up!

Conclusion

There are two ways to be successful, if I can be so dualistic at this point. The first is to try to outmaneuver everyone else in our herd as we compete to reach the same finishing line – shoving each other aside as we, like lemmings, fall off the proverbial cliff of possibility. The second is to devise a new game that we can play together, with others – a game with a shared goal and a game that we can all win. This second approach asks us to be wildly creative, bold, daring, courageous, adventurous, vulnerable, anxious, and honest with ourselves.

We need to be all those things, because there are massive challenges at hand. All around us there are signs of crisis, collapse, and breakdown. And at the same time we are also seeing significant and far reaching breakthroughs. We are learning more about who we are and how our minds work which, in turn, enables us to develop better systems better suited to our needs and capabilities. Yes, we are irrational and we can be greedy. We are also wired to be altruistic, our brains are rewarded for caring, sharing, and helping. We have many forms of intelligence and plasticity in our neural pathways. We can and do learn and evolve.

We are also coming together into a social evolution far beyond any social evolution we have experienced in human history. While we are not in control of that evolution, we are consciously and deliberately contributing to it as we develop new technologies, new social systems, new ways of working together, more effective group processes, and more effective collaborations. We have developed leaderless networks – and are beginning to generate self-awareness within these network organisms. Our businesses are learning how to interoperate as they enter the Social Era (the right antidote to the downsizing they are condemned to as they pass their peak rates of growth). What better way to maintain a sizeable footprint in the world than by including what is outside the organization in what the organization does?

We have developed better ways of seeing ourselves through data collection, formatting, and visualization. It improves our efficiency and makes us smarter about what actions to take as individuals and as collectives.

We can also increasingly act on the values we hold as we can see more clearly what aligns with them. We can see more of what works and we can do more of it.

While these are significant breakthroughs, the world seems to be changing faster than ever. And with more things and information and people being connected, the unpredictability of the complex, adaptive and sometimes even chaotic systems that we are a part of still has us confused and anxious. To navigate all this uncertainty with agility, we need to know what kind of system we are working within so we can select suitable actions and know what to expect from them.

We also need to continue improving our ability to be creative and to innovate. We can't control creativity, but we can create the conditions where creativity can show up. Humans don't perform creativity the way they perform mechanical tasks. We need different incentive systems for these different types of tasks. So game design, applying insights from neuroscience and behavioral economics, can motivate people (you and me) to move in desirable directions together.

Still, there is this huge challenge of uncertainty. Even with small iterations, bold moves, and collective intelligence, the challenges we face are monstrous.

I believe the only way we will make it through these changes is by believing that we will. As Jessica Hagy puts it: "If we don't know that greatness is possible, we won't bother attempting it."

I hope this book has helped you see that greatness might be possible for us. Significant work is being done – and much has been done already – that provides the crucial breakthroughs for a world that works differently than it has in the past. A world that works better because we all participate in it. I dare myself every day to help co-create a thrivable world. I dare you to join me. Dare greatly. Dare to create, innovate, and change. Dare to create more than we consume, because generating value thrills us. Dare to live into a vision of a world that works for you, your loved ones, your community, your organization, and our society. I dare you.

~

Reflecting on the book, I recognize that at the heart of thrivability is gratitude. Not only that. Gratitude is not only *at* the heart, it *is* the heart of thrivability.

I want to invite us all to step into gratitude. From a place of gratitude we can acknowledge the gifts the past offers us. From a place of gratitude, we can move beyond systems that were well designed with the best of our abilities and intentions at the time. From a place of gratitude we can generate new (or evolve newer) systems that better serve our more discerning goals. From a place of gratitude we can adjust our goals based on the feedback we have received on how well our earlier versions served humanity and the (eco)systems we depend on. At the heart of thriving is gratitude to one another for the gifts we bring to the table. Gratitude for the technology that allows us to better understand ourselves and our universe. And gratitude for becoming conscious, albeit irrational, creatures who can play games that delight us. The heart and the soul of thrivability is gratitude. A thriving life stems from gratitude. A thriving organization expresses gratitude. A thriving society and culture breathes gratitude. Yes, I mean that in an airy spiritual way. And yes I mean it in a technical, psychological-wiring way. And finally, I mean it in a practitioner's sense of being witness to, and practicing, gratitude deeply. So, let's be grateful and...

Level up!

Acknowledgements

I met with a man that friends and I have affectionately called the Merlin of our age. He doesn't look like Merlin though. Rather, he looks the part of a well educated Englishman you might find at the University Club or walking out of a business meeting in the financial district. I sat in his Manhattan apartment, drinking coffee with him during an intense two hour conversation. I knew he was over 80 at that time, because I heard he went to burning man – as his friends suggested – for his 80th birthday. At the end of our wide-ranging conversation, he said, "you should write this as a book." So I did. I outlined this book, based on that conversation, as soon as I got back to my friend's place in South Brooklyn. Two months later, I had 3 chapters written.

Okay, maybe not everyone would actually work for two years on a project of this scope after a single conversation in New York. But I am pretty sure several books each year give credit to Napier for nudging them into existence. He is the kind of quiet magical 'leader' that makes things happen in the world without most people even knowing his name. To me, he exemplifies thrivability. He lives in an ongoing state of committed deep curiosity. He plants seeds where he sees sparks of life emerging. He nurtures what takes hold and begins to unfold. He is immensely generative. I hope I can be like Napier someday. And I hope he was right that this book might plant a seed for you and for us.

I want to thank very deeply and humbly my editor, Andrew Carey. He played with me through all the twists and turns of transforming a rough draft of a book into this finished version. He says I made the gem in my mouth. I say he polished it just so. Having worked as an editor, I know just how much the editor does to transform a work into a final product – it is the labor that makes rock into sparkling jewelry delightful to behold.

Much gratitude to the friends who listened and loved me warmly during my breakdowns and breakthroughs in writing this book: Deanna Zandt, Christina Jordan, Kaliya Hamlin, Travis Wellman, Jana Inuit, Manar Hussain, Herman Wagter, Christelle Van Ham, Mushin Schilling, Cameron Burgess, Kimberly Olson, Tracy Gary, and Steve Crandall. I can't possibly list everyone who helped, nudged, prodded, encouraged, and sympathized. It took a network. A big one. Thank you all.

With gratitude to my champions and donors for making the dedication to do this work possible and cheered me on: Herman Wagter, John Hagel, Manar Hussain, Lewis Hoffman, Deanna Zandt, Gerard Senehi, Drake Zimmerman, Amir Baghdadi, Monica Zaucha, Imaginify, Christopher Douglas, Kurt Opprecht, and Todd Hoskins. And most of all to my sister Joan and her husband Jim Jones for giving me shelter for four months of writing.

Thank you to early readers who helped guide and shape the early drafts: Danielle Lanyard, Bernd Nurnberger, Deanna Zandt, Christine Egger, Napier Collyns, Nilofer Merchant, Evonne Heyning, Bo McFarland, Jay Ogilvy, Steve Kammen, Hava Gurevich, Irma Wilson, Nathaniel James, Donnie Maclurcan, and John Hagel (who reordered it).

Index

About the Publisher

Triarchy Press is an independent publisher of new alternative thinking (altThink) about organizations and society – and practical ways to apply that thinking.

Where Jean Russell talks about the deadening effect of 'breakdown thinking' and the world of possibility opened up by 'breakthrough thinking', she exemplifies what we see as the vital difference between conThink (conventional thinking) and the kind of practical hope and wise initiative inspired by altThink.

Other titles from Triarchy Press:

Restoring practical hope and inspiring wise initiative are two of the intentions of International Futures Forum – one of Triarchy's Publishing Partners. IFF's books on designing resilience, transformative innovation in education, Three Horizons thinking and things to do in a conceptual emergency have all been published by Triarchy Press.

One of the most intriguing topics currently being discussed by futurists is the likely future evolution of the human mind. This is a subject addressed in depth by Jack Huber in his 2013 title *The Future of the Mind*.

Planning for the future is also a highly technical matter and one of the longest-established and most highly valued approaches is Scenario Planning. *Facing the Fold* brings together a collection of the best essays on the subject by one of its leading proponents, James (Jay) Ogilvy.

Scenario Planning is one of several techniques discussed by Stephen Millett in his guide to forecasting and planning. *Managing the Future* offers a straightforward and pragmatic approach to strategic planning in business. It takes an honest look at the limitations of forecasting, and shows how managers can best use a variety of futuring methods, including scenarios, horizon scanning and trend monitoring.

Details of all these titles (as well as Thought Papers and Idioticon entries) can be found at www.triarchypress.net/the-future

www.triarchypress.net

About the Author

Jean M. Russell is:

- **a facilitator and coach.** She takes entrepreneurs, social innovators, and business builders on tours of network culture and helps clients navigate the crucial questions of how best to create, nurture and motivate teams and networks to develop healthy and productive relationships and innovative collaborations.

- **a social ecosystem designer.** She is on a quest to catalyze group productivity and has been facilitating strategy retreats, conferences, and workshops in North America, Europe, and Australia since 2007. She brings to her facilitation a keen understanding of social network analysis, motivation, influence, behavior patterns, group dynamics, and culture change. Jean often custom designs participatory structures for group engagement that evoke play to achieve purpose.

Jean is a founder of the thrivability movement and, as an expert on collective thriving, she curated *Thrivability: A Collaborative Sketch* in 2010 with 65 inspiring people. She received an 'honorable mention' on the Enrich List of the top 200 people enriching our path to a sustainable future.

> *"If you find yourself on the ragged edge of innovation and change, and are seeking a guide to help navigate elusive territory where rules are not fully formed, you really ought to engage Jean. Jean has an unusually deep awareness and clear vision of the underlying social dynamics of a group. Her technical acumen and web savvy bring a relevant context to technology execs, while her passion for thrivability makes her an excellent guide to sustainable business leaders. Her manner is a mix of deep empathy and a tough-minded insight that will soothe your anxiety while heightening your understanding of a difficult situation. I strongly recommend this experience for someone who wants to evolve into the next wave of leadership."*
> Greg Berry, Managing Director & Co-Founder, Impact Hub Boulder

Find her at:
www.jeanmrussell.com
www.thrivable.net
@thrivable
facebook.com/JeanMRussell

Lightning Source UK Ltd.
Milton Keynes UK
UKOW03f0741041213

222329UK00002B/47/P